Bold Operations

Building the Foundation of Strategic Excellence in Restaurants

By Jim Taylor

For more information or to contact us directly:
https://www.benchmarksixty.com/

ISBN - eBook: 978-1-998585-42-7

<u>DISCLAIMER</u>

The content provided in this book is designed to provide helpful information on the subjects discussed. This book is not meant to be used, nor should it be used, to diagnose or treat any medical condition. The claims in this book are theoretical and to be used for illustrative purposes only. The publisher and the authors are not responsible for any actions you take or do not take as a result of reading this book and are not liable for any damages or negative consequences from action or inaction to any person reading or following the information in this book. References are provided for informational purposes only and do not constitute endorsement of any websites or other sources. Readers should also be aware that the websites listed in this book may change or become obsolete.

Table of Content

Dedication

This book is dedicated to my incredible wife Jen, and my daughter Makena.

Jen, you are the light of my life. You challenge me to be better every day, and the care you show for people every day is an ongoing example of how every person should act. Your support for me will always show me that nothing is out of reach, and I can accomplish anything. I love you.

Makena, becoming your Dad changed me forever in the best ways possible. I can only hope that I make you as happy as you make me, and I can't wait to see the person you continue to become. Keep being you. I love you.

Introduction

The Importance of Strategic Management in the Restaurant Industry

The restaurant industry is a dynamic and challenging landscape, one that demands constant adaptation and innovation to stay ahead of the curve. In an environment where high turnover rates, employee mental health concerns, and razor-thin profit margins are the norm, strategic management isn't just a luxury—it's an absolute necessity for survival and success. The challenges faced by restaurant owners and managers today are multifaceted and complex, requiring a nuanced approach that goes beyond the traditional methods of running an eatery.

Consider the staggering reality of employee turnover in the restaurant industry. With rates that often exceed 100% annually, restaurants are constantly caught in a costly cycle of hiring and training new staff. This revolving door not only drains financial resources but also erodes team cohesion, customer service quality, and overall operational efficiency. The financial impact is severe, with some estimates suggesting that replacing a single employee can cost a restaurant upwards of $5,000 when factoring in recruitment, training, and lost productivity during the transition period.

Compounding this issue is the often-overlooked aspect of employee mental health. The fast-paced, high-stress environment of a restaurant can take a significant toll on workers' well-being. Long hours, irregular schedules, and the constant pressure to perform in customer-facing roles create a perfect storm for burnout and mental health challenges. These factors not only contribute to the high turnover rates but also impact the quality of service and the overall atmosphere of the establishment. A restaurant that fails to address these concerns may find itself trapped in a vicious cycle of dissatisfied employees leading to dissatisfied customers, ultimately threatening the very foundation of the business.

Profitability, the lifeblood of any business, presents its own set of hurdles in the restaurant industry. With food costs rising, labor expenses increasing, and customers becoming more price-sensitive, maintaining healthy profit margins requires a delicate balancing act. The traditional approach of simply raising prices or cutting costs is no longer sufficient in today's competitive market. Restaurants must find innovative ways to increase efficiency, maximize revenue, and create value for customers without sacrificing quality or employee well-being.

These challenges might seem daunting, but they also present an unprecedented opportunity for those willing to embrace strategic management principles. By addressing these issues head-on, restaurant owners and managers can not only survive but thrive in this competitive landscape. This book is designed to be your guide through this complex terrain, offering practical solutions and innovative strategies that go beyond the conventional wisdom of restaurant management.

Throughout these pages, you'll discover a wealth of insights drawn from years of experience in the trenches of the restaurant industry. We'll explore cutting-edge approaches to reducing turnover that go beyond simple retention tactics, delving into the core of what makes employees want to stay and grow with your organization. You'll learn how to create a workplace culture that not only attracts top talent but nurtures and develops it, turning your restaurant into a beacon for skilled professionals in the industry.

We'll tackle the critical issue of employee mental health with sensitivity and practicality, providing you with tools and strategies to support your team's well-being without compromising operational efficiency. From implementing flexible scheduling systems to creating open channels of communication, you'll gain a comprehensive understanding of how to build a resilient and motivated workforce that can weather the storms of the restaurant business.

Profitability will be approached from multiple angles, combining time-tested financial management techniques with innovative approaches to menu engineering, cost control, and revenue optimization. You'll learn how to leverage technology to streamline operations, reduce waste, and enhance the customer experience in ways that directly impact your bottom line. We'll explore the power of data-driven decision-making, showing you how to use metrics and analytics to fine-tune every aspect of your business for maximum efficiency and profitability.

But this book is more than just a collection of strategies and tactics. It's a paradigm shift in how we think about restaurant management. Throughout these chapters, you'll be challenged to question long-held assumptions about the industry and to reimagine what's possible for your business. We'll introduce you to unique concepts and metrics that will change the way you evaluate success, from employee workload optimization to holistic business productivity measures that capture the true health of your operation.

As you journey through this book, you'll find that each chapter builds upon the last, creating a comprehensive framework for strategic management in the restaurant industry. The insights and strategies presented here are not theoretical abstractions but practical, actionable steps that you can implement in your business immediately. Whether you're a seasoned restaurateur looking to take your operation to the next level or a new manager seeking to build a solid foundation for success, this book offers something valuable for everyone in the industry.

The path ahead may be challenging, but it's also filled with incredible opportunities for those who are prepared to seize them. By embracing the principles of strategic management outlined in this book, you'll be equipped to navigate the complexities of the restaurant industry with confidence and vision. You'll learn how to create a workplace that not only retains top talent but inspires loyalty and innovation. You'll discover how to build a business that's not just profitable but sustainable and resilient in the face of industry challenges.

As we embark on this journey together, remember that the strategies and insights shared in these pages are not just about improving your business—they're about transforming the restaurant industry as a whole. By implementing these ideas, you'll be part of a movement towards a more sustainable, employee-centric, and profitable future for restaurants everywhere. The challenges we face are significant, but so are the rewards for those who rise to meet them. Let's turn the page and begin the transformation of your restaurant and, by extension, the entire industry.

My Journey in the Restaurant Industry

The restaurant industry has been an integral part of my life since childhood. My parents, recognizing the value of early exposure to hospitality, taught me to open wine bottles for their Christmas parties – a seemingly small task that would later spark a lifelong passion. This early introduction to the world of service and entertainment laid the foundation for what would become a deeply rooted love affair with the restaurant business, shaping not only my career but my entire perspective on the industry.

As a teenager, I took my first official steps into the restaurant world, and the experience was nothing short of transformative. The pulsating energy of a busy kitchen, the synchronized dance of servers weaving through tables, and the satisfaction of creating memorable experiences for guests – it all captivated me instantly. However, amidst the exhilaration, I couldn't help but notice a troubling undercurrent: the way people were treated and spoken to often left a bitter taste. It was clear that the industry I loved had room for improvement, particularly in how it valued and nurtured its most precious resource – its people.

At the age of 19, I joined a large corporate restaurant group, marking the beginning of a 20-year journey that would take me across the country and expose me to countless facets of the business. This experience proved to be an invaluable crucible for learning and growth. Thrust into management roles early on, often overseeing staff who were older and more experienced than myself, I quickly realized that the key to effective leadership lay in breaking away from the harsh, authoritarian management styles I had witnessed. By approaching my team with respect and empathy, I discovered that they were far more responsive and motivated, setting the stage for a management philosophy that would define my career.

As I progressed through various roles, from general restaurant management to overseeing multi-unit operations and spearheading new business initiatives, I honed my skills in team building, recruitment, and organizational alignment. The challenge of opening new establishments in unfamiliar markets taught me the importance of quickly assembling and motivating high-performing teams. These experiences underscored the critical nature of selecting the right management personnel, fostering their growth, and creating an environment where they could thrive and drive the business forward.

In 2015, faced with rapidly escalating costs across the industry – from skyrocketing wages to volatile food prices – I recognized the need for a paradigm shift in how we approached the restaurant business model. This realization led me to build a team dedicated to reimagining our approach to data analysis and operational strategy. We had gone into metrics that had previously been overlooked, such as overall business productivity, menu dollar contribution, and variance to theoretical cost. Perhaps most significantly, we introduced the concept of "employee workload" to the restaurant industry, drawing inspiration from professional sports' approach to athlete management.

This innovative perspective on workforce management aimed to protect our staff from burnout and injury, much like how sports teams safeguard their athletes. By carefully monitoring and managing employee workload, we sought to create a more sustainable and productive work environment, ultimately enhancing both employee satisfaction and business performance. This approach not only improved our operations but also set the stage for a broader industry transformation.

The culmination of these experiences and insights led to the founding of Benchmark Sixty Restaurant Services in 2020. Despite launching in the midst of a global pandemic, our mission to support and revolutionize the restaurant industry resonated strongly with businesses struggling to navigate unprecedented challenges. Over the past four years, we've had the privilege of collaborating with hundreds of restaurant groups, helping them to reimagine their operations, prioritize their people, and adapt to a rapidly changing landscape.

Our journey has been marked by strategic partnerships with suppliers, technology companies, educational institutions, and industry leaders, all united in the goal of elevating the restaurant industry. These collaborations have not only expanded our reach but also enriched our understanding of the diverse challenges facing restaurants today. In 2022, I was deeply honored to be inducted into the Culinary Institute of America's "Society of Fellows," a recognition that underscored the impact of our work. Regular speaking engagements at events like the Restaurant's Canada "RC Show" have provided platforms to share our vision and strategies with a wider audience. Being named to Vancouver BC's list of top 100 innovators in 2023 further validated our approach and the positive changes we've been able to effect in the industry.

This journey, from a child learning the basics of hospitality to leading an organization at the forefront of restaurant industry innovation, has been both challenging and immensely rewarding. Each step along the way has reinforced my belief in the power of compassionate leadership, data-driven decision making, and the importance of prioritizing the well-being of those who are the heart and soul of our industry – the employees. As we continue to evolve and adapt to new challenges, I remain committed to fostering a more sustainable, equitable, and thriving restaurant ecosystem for all.

What You Will Learn

The restaurant industry is a complex and challenging environment, fraught with unique obstacles that can make or break even the most promising establishments. In this book, you'll gain invaluable insights into three critical areas that can dramatically impact your restaurant's success: reducing turnover, enhancing employee well-being, and driving profitability. These aren't just buzzwords or fleeting trends; they're the foundational pillars upon which thriving restaurants are built in today's competitive landscape.

Turnover in the restaurant industry has long been a thorn in the side of owners and managers, with rates often exceeding 70% annually. This constant churn of staff not only disrupts operations but also bleeds your bottom line dry through increased training costs and lost productivity. We'll go deep into the root causes of this pervasive issue, exploring innovative strategies that go beyond the standard "competitive pay and benefits" approach. You'll learn how to create a work environment that not only attracts top talent but also nurtures and retains it, transforming your restaurant into a beacon of stability in an otherwise turbulent industry.

Employee well-being is intrinsically linked to your restaurant's performance, yet it's an aspect that's often overlooked in the hustle and bustle of daily operations. The high-stress nature of restaurant work, combined with long hours and often unpredictable schedules, can take a significant toll on your staff's mental and physical health. We'll explore comprehensive approaches to fostering a workplace that prioritizes employee wellness, from implementing flexible scheduling systems to creating support networks within your team. You'll discover how investing in your employees' well-being can lead to increased productivity, improved customer service, and ultimately, a more profitable business.

Profitability is the lifeblood of any business, but in the restaurant industry, razor-thin margins leave little room for error. Traditional approaches to boosting profits often focus on cutting costs or raising prices, but we'll explore more nuanced and sustainable methods. You'll learn how to leverage data-driven insights to optimize your menu, streamline operations, and identify hidden opportunities for revenue growth. We'll introduce you to unique metrics such as employee workload and business productivity, providing you with a fresh perspective on how to measure and improve your restaurant's performance.

What sets this book apart is its focus on practical, actionable strategies that you can implement in your restaurant immediately. We won't waste your time with theoretical concepts that sound good on paper but fall flat in the real world. Instead, you'll find step-by-step guides, real-world examples, and concrete tools that have been battle-tested in restaurants across the country. Whether you're struggling with high turnover, looking to improve your team's morale, or seeking ways to boost your bottom line, you'll find targeted solutions that address your specific challenges.

Throughout the book, we'll challenge conventional wisdom and industry norms, encouraging you to think differently about your restaurant and its potential. You'll learn why many common practices in the industry are outdated or counterproductive, and how embracing new approaches can give you a competitive edge. We'll explore how technology can be leveraged to streamline operations, enhance customer experiences, and provide valuable insights into your business. From advanced scheduling software that optimizes staff allocation to data analytics tools that help you make informed decisions; you'll discover how to harness the power of technology to drive your restaurant's success.

One of the most valuable aspects of this book is its introduction to unique metrics that can provide deeper insights into your restaurant's performance. Employee workload, for instance, goes beyond simple labor cost percentages to help you understand how efficiently your staff is being utilized. Business productivity metrics will show you not just how much you're selling, but how effectively you're converting inputs into outputs. These advanced measures will give you a more nuanced understanding of your restaurant's operations, allowing you to make more informed decisions and implement targeted improvements.

By the time you finish this book, you'll have a comprehensive toolkit for transforming your restaurant into a more profitable, stable, and employee-friendly establishment. You'll understand how to create a positive workplace culture that attracts and retains top talent, implement strategies that boost your bottom line without sacrificing quality or employee well-being, and leverage data and technology to stay ahead of the curve. Most importantly, you'll be equipped with the knowledge and skills to adapt to the ever-changing landscape of the restaurant industry, ensuring your business not only survives but thrives in the years to come.

Overview of Chapters

The journey through this book is designed to revolutionize your approach to restaurant management, offering a comprehensive roadmap for success in an industry known for its challenges. Each chapter builds upon the last, creating a cohesive strategy that addresses the most pressing issues facing restaurant owners and managers today. From reducing turnover rates to boosting profitability, the insights shared are both practical and transformative, backed by years of industry experience and data-driven analysis.

We begin by delving deep into the heart of strategic management in the restaurant industry. This foundational chapter explores the unique challenges that set restaurants apart from other businesses, examining how traditional management practices often fall short in this dynamic environment. You'll gain a nuanced understanding of why restaurants require a specialized approach, setting the stage for the innovative strategies presented throughout the book. This chapter doesn't just highlight problems; it offers concrete solutions, providing you with tools to assess your current management style and identify areas for immediate improvement.

People take center stage in the next chapter, where we tackle one of the industry's most persistent challenges: employee turnover. Through a combination of case studies and actionable advice, you'll learn how to create a work environment that not only attracts top talent but also encourages long-term commitment. This section goes beyond surface-level solutions, diving into the psychology of employee satisfaction and the tangible benefits of investing in your staff. You'll discover how to implement retention strategies that work, from innovative training programs to career development opportunities that keep your team engaged and loyal.

In an era where technology is reshaping every aspect of the restaurant experience, our chapter on tech integration is crucial for staying competitive. We explore how cutting-edge solutions can streamline operations, enhance customer experiences, and provide valuable data insights. From point-of-sale systems that offer real-time analytics to AI-powered inventory management, you'll learn how to leverage technology to make informed decisions and drive profitability. This chapter provides a step-by-step guide to assessing your current tech stack, identifying gaps, and implementing new solutions that align with your business goals.

The importance of workplace culture cannot be overstated, and our dedicated chapter on this topic provides a blueprint for creating an environment where employees thrive. We examine the elements that contribute to a positive culture, from leadership styles to communication practices, and how these factors directly impact your bottom line. You'll learn strategies for fostering a sense of belonging and purpose among your staff, leading to increased productivity and customer satisfaction. This chapter also addresses the unique challenges of maintaining culture across multiple locations or franchises, ensuring consistency in your brand experience.

Financial management in the restaurant industry requires a specialized approach, and our chapter on this topic provides the tools you need to navigate the complexities of restaurant finances. From menu pricing strategies to cost control measures, you'll gain insights into maximizing profitability without compromising quality. We introduce unique metrics specifically tailored to the restaurant industry, allowing you to track performance in ways that traditional financial measures might miss. This chapter empowers you to make data-driven decisions that positively impact your bottom line, even in the face of rising costs and narrow margins.

The book concludes with a forward-looking chapter on innovation and adaptation in the restaurant industry. We explore emerging trends and technologies that are poised to reshape the dining landscape, from ghost kitchens to sustainable practices. This section provides a framework for staying ahead of the curve, helping you anticipate and prepare for future challenges. You'll learn how to foster a culture of innovation within your organization, encouraging creativity and experimentation while managing risk. This chapter ensures that the strategies you've learned throughout the book remain relevant and effective in an ever-changing industry.

Throughout these chapters, you'll find a consistent focus on practical, actionable advice. Each section includes detailed implementation strategies, potential pitfalls to avoid, and metrics for measuring success. Real-world examples illustrate how these concepts have been successfully applied in various restaurant settings, from small independent eateries to large chains. By the end of this book, you'll have a comprehensive toolkit for transforming your restaurant's operations, culture, and profitability. The insights gained will not only help you navigate current challenges but also position your business for long-term success in an industry that demands constant adaptation and innovation.

Understanding the High Turnover Rate in Restaurants

Problem Introduction

The restaurant industry, a vibrant and dynamic sector of our economy, faces a persistent challenge that threatens its very foundation: an alarmingly high turnover rate. This revolving door of employees, spinning faster than a busy kitchen's order wheel, has become an accepted norm in the culinary world, but it's time we take a closer look at this phenomenon and understand its far-reaching implications. The constant flux of staff doesn't just disrupt daily operations; it erodes the very essence of what makes a restaurant successful - consistency, quality, and the human touch that turns first-time diners into loyal patrons.

To truly grasp the magnitude of this issue, we need to dive deep into the numbers that paint a stark picture of the industry's retention struggles. According to recent studies, the average turnover rate in the restaurant sector hovers around a staggering 75%, with some establishments experiencing rates as high as 100% or more annually. This means that, in many cases, restaurants are essentially replacing their entire workforce every single year. The financial burden of this turnover is equally jaw-dropping, with estimates suggesting that replacing a single employee can cost a restaurant anywhere from $3,000 to $5,000, factoring in recruitment, training, and lost productivity during the transition period.

But what's driving this carousel of coming and going? The factors contributing to high turnover in the restaurant industry are as varied as the menu items in a fine dining establishment. At the forefront is the nature of the work itself - long hours, physically demanding tasks, and the relentless pressure of service rushes can wear down even the most passionate culinary professionals. Add to this the often-unpredictable scheduling, which can wreak havoc on work-life balance, and you have a recipe for employee burnout. Many workers, particularly those in entry-level positions, view restaurant jobs as temporary steppingstones rather than long-term career paths, further exacerbating the turnover issue.

The hierarchical structure typical in many kitchens and dining rooms can also contribute to high turnover rates. The traditional "brigade" system, while efficient for task delegation, can create a high-pressure environment where communication breakdowns and interpersonal conflicts are common. When employees feel undervalued or see limited opportunities for growth and advancement within their current role, they're more likely to seek greener pastures. This constant churn not only impacts the bottom line but also erodes the institutional knowledge and team cohesion that are crucial for delivering exceptional dining experiences.

To compound these challenges, the restaurant industry often grapples with a perception problem. Many view food service jobs as temporary or less prestigious than other careers, leading to a constant influx of transient workers who may not be fully invested in their roles. This perception can be a self-fulfilling prophecy, as it influences how management approaches employee development and retention strategies. When owners and managers operate under the assumption that high turnover is inevitable, they may inadvertently create conditions that perpetuate the cycle, failing to invest in the training, support, and career development that could encourage long-term commitment from their staff.

Understanding these multifaceted drivers of turnover is the first step toward addressing the issue. It's crucial for restaurant owners and managers to recognize that while some level of turnover may be inherent to the industry, the current rates are unsustainable and detrimental to long-term success. By acknowledging the problem and its root causes, we can begin to craft targeted strategies that not only reduce turnover but also create a more stable, satisfied, and productive workforce. The challenge lies in balancing the unique demands of the restaurant environment with the needs and aspirations of the individuals who make up its workforce.

Employee Satisfaction and Retention

Employee satisfaction stands as the cornerstone of a thriving restaurant business, serving as the invisible force that propels establishments towards success or pushes them into a downward spiral of constant turnover and diminished quality. In an industry where the human element is paramount, understanding and nurturing job satisfaction isn't just a feel-good initiative—it's a critical business strategy that can make the difference between a restaurant that merely survives and one that truly flourishes. The importance of job satisfaction extends far beyond the immediate mood of your staff; it permeates every aspect of your operation, from the quality of food preparation to the warmth of customer interactions, ultimately impacting your bottom line in ways both subtle and profound.

At its core, job satisfaction in the restaurant industry is about creating an environment where employees feel valued, supported, and motivated to give their best. This involves a multifaceted approach that addresses both the tangible and intangible aspects of the work experience. One of the most effective strategies for enhancing employee engagement and loyalty is to implement a robust feedback system that not only allows workers to voice their concerns and suggestions but also demonstrates that management is actively listening and responding to those inputs. This can be achieved through regular one-on-one meetings, anonymous suggestion boxes, or even digital platforms that facilitate ongoing dialogue between staff and management.

Another crucial element in fostering job satisfaction is providing clear paths for growth and development within the organization. In an industry often perceived as offering limited career prospects, showcasing potential advancement opportunities can be a game-changer. This might involve creating a structured mentorship program where seasoned staff members guide newer employees, offering cross-training opportunities that allow staff to develop diverse skill sets, or even implementing a points-based system that rewards employees for acquiring new skills or certifications. By demonstrating a commitment to your employees' long-term growth, you not only improve their current job satisfaction but also increase the likelihood that they'll view your restaurant as a place where they can build a fulfilling career rather than just a temporary stopover.

Recognition and appreciation play an equally vital role in maintaining high levels of employee satisfaction and retention. While monetary rewards are certainly appreciated, non-financial recognition can be just as impactful when done thoughtfully and consistently. Consider implementing an "Employee of the Month" program that goes beyond a simple plaque on the wall—perhaps offering the winner a prime parking spot, an extra day off, or the ability to choose their preferred shifts for the following month. Regular staff appreciation events, such as team dinners or outings, can also foster a sense of camaraderie and belonging that transcends the day-to-day work environment.

Work-life balance, often overlooked in the demanding restaurant industry, is another critical factor in employee satisfaction and retention. While the nature of the business often requires irregular hours and weekend work, there are still ways to promote better balance. Implementing a fair and transparent scheduling system that takes into account employee preferences and needs can go a long way in reducing stress and burnout. Consider offering flexible shift options where possible, such as split shifts or compressed workweeks, to accommodate diverse lifestyles and commitments. Additionally, providing adequate time off and encouraging employees to use their vacation days can help prevent burnout and show that you value their well-being beyond their role in the restaurant.

Investing in the right tools and technology can also significantly impact employee satisfaction by making their jobs easier and more efficient. This could mean upgrading to a more user-friendly point-of-sale system, implementing inventory management software that streamlines ordering and stock-taking processes, or even providing tablets for servers to input orders directly at the table. By reducing frustration and increasing efficiency, these technological improvements not only make the work experience more enjoyable but also empower employees to provide better service to customers.

Creating a culture of continuous learning and improvement is another powerful strategy for enhancing employee engagement and loyalty. Regular training sessions that go beyond the basics of food safety and customer service can keep staff engaged and invested in their roles. These might include wine tasting workshops for servers, advanced culinary techniques for kitchen staff, or even broader skills like conflict resolution or time management. By investing in your employees' professional development, you're not only improving their current performance but also signaling your commitment to their long-term success within your organization.

Finally, fostering a sense of ownership and pride in the restaurant's success can be a powerful motivator for employees at all levels. This might involve sharing key performance metrics with staff, soliciting their input on menu changes or promotional events, or even implementing a profit-sharing program that directly ties the restaurant's success. When employees feel that they have a stake in the outcome, they're more likely to go above and beyond in their roles, leading to improved performance and higher job satisfaction.

Implementing these strategies requires a concerted effort and ongoing commitment from management, but the payoff in terms of reduced turnover, improved service quality, and overall business success can be substantial. By prioritizing employee satisfaction and retention, restaurant owners and managers can create a positive cycle where satisfied employees deliver exceptional experiences, leading to satisfied customers and a thriving business. In an industry known for its challenges, making your restaurant a place where people want to work—

not just a place where they have to work—can be your most powerful competitive advantage.

Competition and Benefits

In the fast-paced world of restaurants, where the sizzle of pans and the clinking of plates create a symphony of culinary delight, there's an underlying melody that often goes unheard - the importance of competition and benefits. This crucial aspect of restaurant management can make the difference between a thriving establishment with loyal staff and a revolving door of employees that leaves both customers and owners dizzy. The restaurant industry, known for its high-energy atmosphere and creative spirit, has long grappled with the challenge of attracting and retaining top talent in a field where turnover rates can reach dizzying heights, sometimes exceeding 70% annually.

To truly understand the landscape of competition and benefits in the restaurant industry, we must first go into the current standards that shape employee expectations and employer offerings. Traditionally, the industry has been characterized by lower base wages, particularly for front-of-house staff who rely heavily on tips. However, this model is increasingly being scrutinized and reimagined as restaurants seek to create more stable and appealing work environments. The baseline for wages varies significantly depending on location, restaurant type, and position, but it's crucial for owners and managers to stay informed about not just the legal minimum wage requirements but also the competitive rates in their specific market.

A comprehensive analysis of industry standards reveals that forward-thinking establishments are moving beyond the bare minimum. They're crafting packages that include not just competitive hourly rates or salaries but also performance-based incentives, profit-sharing programs, and even equity options for key positions. These innovative approaches serve a dual purpose: they motivate employees to invest in the success of the restaurant while also providing a tangible pathway for career growth and financial stability. For instance, implementing a tiered wage system that rewards longevity and skill development can significantly reduce turnover by giving staff a clear trajectory for advancement within the organization.

When structuring a competitive package, it's essential to consider the holistic needs of your employees. This means looking beyond the paycheck and exploring benefits that can make a real difference in their lives. Health insurance, often seen as a luxury in the restaurant industry, is becoming increasingly important to workers across all sectors. Offering even a basic health plan can set your establishment apart and demonstrate a commitment to your staff's well-being. Additionally, paid time off, including sick days and vacation time, can help prevent burnout and show that you value work-life balance - a concept that's gaining traction even in the traditionally demanding restaurant environment.

Another aspect of benefits that's often overlooked but can be highly impactful is professional development opportunities. Investing in your staff's growth through training programs, workshops, or even tuition assistance for culinary or management courses can foster loyalty and improve the overall skill level of your team. This not only benefits the individual employees but also elevates the quality of service and cuisine your restaurant can offer, creating a positive feedback loop that enhances both employee satisfaction and customer experience.

In crafting your strategy, it's crucial to maintain transparency and fairness. Clearly communicate your pay structure and the criteria for raises or bonuses to all employees. This openness can prevent misunderstandings and foster a sense of trust between management and staff. Consider implementing a regular review process where employees can discuss their performance, providing a structured opportunity for feedback and growth. By doing so, you create a culture of open dialogue and continuous improvement that can significantly boost morale and retention.

It's worth noting that while competition is essential, it's not a silver bullet for all retention issues. The most effective strategies combine fair pay with a positive work environment, opportunities for growth, and a strong sense of purpose. Encourage your management team to regularly solicit feedback from staff about their needs and aspirations. This information can be invaluable in fine-tuning your package to ensure it truly resonates with your team.

Implementing these changes may seem daunting, especially for smaller establishments or those operating on tight margins. However, the long-term benefits of reduced turnover, increased productivity, and improved customer satisfaction can far outweigh the initial investment. Start by analyzing your current structure and identifying areas for improvement. Set realistic goals for enhancing your offerings over time and be creative in finding ways to add value for your employees that don't necessarily require a large financial outlay.

Remember, in the competitive landscape of the restaurant industry, your staff is your most valuable asset. By prioritizing competition and benefits, you're not just filling positions - you're building a team of dedicated professionals who are invested in your restaurant's success. This approach can transform your establishment from just another workplace into a career destination, where talented individuals aspire to work and grow. In doing so, you'll not only reduce turnover but also create a vibrant, skilled, and loyal workforce that can elevate your restaurant to new heights of culinary excellence and customer satisfaction.

Work Environment and Culture

The restaurant industry is notorious for its high-pressure environments, long hours, and demanding customers. These factors can contribute significantly to employee burnout and, consequently, high turnover rates. However, creating a positive work environment and fostering a supportive culture can be a game-changer in retaining valuable staff members and reducing the costly cycle of hiring and training new employees. A well-crafted workplace culture acts as the invisible glue that binds teams together, promotes job satisfaction, and ultimately leads to improved customer experiences.

At the heart of a positive work environment lies open communication. Establishing clear channels for feedback, concerns, and ideas allows employees to feel heard and valued. This can be achieved through regular team meetings, one-on-one check-ins with managers, or even anonymous suggestion boxes. The key is to create an atmosphere where staff members feel comfortable expressing themselves without fear of repercussion. When employees know their voices matter, they're more likely to invest emotionally in their work and the success of the restaurant.

Recognition and appreciation play crucial roles in building a supportive culture. Implementing a structured recognition program can significantly boost morale and motivation. This doesn't necessarily mean lavish rewards; sometimes, a simple acknowledgment of a job well done can make all the difference. Consider instituting an "Employee of the Month" program, offering small bonuses for exceptional performance, or even just making it a point to verbally praise staff members in front of their peers. These gestures, while seemingly small, can have a profound impact on how valued employees feel in their roles.

Professional development opportunities are another vital component of a positive work environment. Many restaurant workers view their jobs as temporary steppingstones, but offering clear paths for growth and advancement can change this perception. Implement a structured training program that allows employees to learn new skills and take on additional responsibilities. This could include cross-training in different roles, offering management training to promising team members, or even sponsoring external courses related to the culinary arts or hospitality management. By investing in your employees' futures, you're not only improving their skills but also fostering loyalty and commitment to your establishment.

Work-life balance is a concept that's often overlooked in the demanding world of restaurants, but it's crucial for long-term employee satisfaction and retention. While the nature of the industry often requires long and irregular hours, there are ways to mitigate the impact on your staff's personal lives. Implement fair scheduling practices that give employees adequate notice of their shifts and try to accommodate personal commitments when possible. Consider offering flexible scheduling options or even compressed workweeks where appropriate. Additionally, ensure that your staff has access to proper break times and areas during their shifts, allowing them to recharge and maintain their energy throughout busy service periods.

Team building activities can significantly contribute to a positive work culture by fostering camaraderie and mutual respect among staff members. Organize regular events outside of work hours, such as staff dinners, cooking competitions, or even volunteer activities in the local community. These shared experiences create bonds between employees that extend beyond the workplace, leading to improved communication and collaboration during busy shifts. They provide opportunities for staff to interact with management in a more relaxed setting, breaking down hierarchical barriers and promoting a sense of unity across all levels of the organization.

Creating a diverse and inclusive environment is essential in today's restaurant industry. Actively seek to build a team that represents a variety of backgrounds, experiences, and perspectives. This diversity not only enriches the workplace culture but also can lead to innovative ideas and improved problem-solving. Implement clear anti-discrimination policies and provide training on cultural sensitivity and unconscious bias. Celebrate the diversity within your team by organizing cultural exchange events or featuring dishes from different culinary traditions on your menu. When employees feel that their unique identities are respected and valued, they're more likely to form a deep connection with their workplace and colleagues.

Physical workspace design can have a significant impact on employee morale and productivity. While the constraints of a restaurant kitchen may limit extensive modifications, small changes can make a big difference. Ensure that workstations are ergonomically designed to reduce physical strain during long shifts. Improve lighting in both front and back-of-house areas to create a more pleasant atmosphere. If space allows, designate a comfortable break area where staff can relax and recharge. Even simple additions like plants or artwork can help create a more inviting environment. By showing that you care about the physical comfort of your employees, you demonstrate a commitment to their well-being that goes beyond just their job performance.

Transparency in decision-making processes can foster trust and engagement among your staff. When implementing new policies or making significant changes to operations, involve your employees in the process. Seek their input, explain the reasoning behind decisions, and be open to feedback. This approach not only leads to better-informed decisions but also helps employees feel like valued contributors to the restaurant's success. Regular staff meetings or newsletters can be effective tools for keeping everyone informed about the restaurant's performance, upcoming events, or industry trends. When employees understand the bigger picture, they're more likely to align their efforts with the restaurant's goals and feel a sense of ownership in its success.

Implementing these strategies to improve your work environment and culture requires consistent effort and commitment from all levels of management. It's not a one-time fix but an ongoing process of evaluation and adjustment. Regularly survey your employees to gauge the effectiveness of your initiatives and identify areas for improvement. Be prepared to adapt your approach based on feedback and changing needs. Remember, the investment you make in creating a positive work environment will pay dividends in reduced turnover costs, improved customer service, and ultimately, a more successful and sustainable restaurant business.

Leadership and Management Practices

The impact of leadership and management practices on turnover rates in the restaurant industry cannot be overstated. In an environment where the pressure is high and the margins are thin, the way managers interact with their staff can make the difference between a cohesive team that sticks together through thick and thin and a revolving door of employees. Effective leadership in the restaurant sector goes beyond simply delegating tasks and monitoring performance; it requires a nuanced understanding of human psychology, a commitment to fostering a positive work environment, and the ability to inspire and motivate a diverse group of individuals.

At its core, effective restaurant management is about creating a sense of purpose and belonging among staff members. This begins with clear communication of expectations and goals, not just for the restaurant as a whole, but for each individual role within the organization. When employees understand how their work contributes to the bigger picture, they're more likely to feel invested in the success of the business. Managers who take the time to explain the 'why' behind tasks and decisions, rather than simply issuing orders, cultivate a culture of understanding and mutual respect.

One of the most critical aspects of leadership in the restaurant industry is the ability to lead by example. In a fast-paced environment where every second counts, managers who are willing to roll up their sleeves and work alongside their staff during busy periods or emergencies earn respect and loyalty. This hands-on approach not only helps during crunch times but also gives leaders a firsthand understanding of the challenges their team faces daily. By experiencing these challenges personally, managers can make more informed decisions about process improvements and resource allocation, further demonstrating their commitment to the team's success and well-being.

Recognition and feedback play a crucial role in employee retention and satisfaction. Effective managers in the restaurant industry understand the power of timely and specific praise. Instead of generic compliments, they take note of particular instances where an employee has excelled – perhaps a server who handled a difficult customer with exceptional grace, or a line cook who maintained quality during an unexpectedly busy shift. By acknowledging these specific contributions, managers reinforce positive behaviors and make employees feel valued as individuals, not just cogs in a machine.

Equally important is the ability to provide constructive feedback in a way that motivates rather than demoralizes. The best managers in the restaurant industry approach correction as an opportunity for growth and learning, not punishment. They create a safe space for employees to make mistakes and learn from them, fostering an environment where continuous improvement is the norm. This approach not only helps retain staff by showing investment in their professional development but also leads to a higher quality of service and food, benefiting the restaurant as a whole.

Another key aspect of effective leadership in restaurants is the ability to manage stress and maintain composure under pressure. The restaurant environment is inherently stressful, with peak hours that can push even the most seasoned professionals to their limits. Leaders who can remain calm and focused during these high-pressure situations set the tone for the entire team. By modeling stress management techniques and maintaining a positive attitude even when things go wrong, managers can create a more resilient workforce that's better equipped to handle the ups and downs of the industry.

Flexibility and adaptability are also crucial traits for restaurant managers. The industry is constantly evolving, with new trends, technologies, and customer expectations emerging all the time. Effective leaders stay ahead of these changes, continuously educating themselves and their team. They're open to new ideas from staff at all levels, recognizing that innovation can come from anywhere. This openness not only helps the restaurant stay competitive but also gives employees a sense of ownership and involvement in the business's success.

Perhaps one of the most overlooked aspects of effective restaurant management is the ability to create and maintain a fair and transparent work environment. This includes everything from scheduling practices to promotion opportunities. Managers who take the time to understand their employees' needs and preferences when it comes to shifts and who communicate clearly about how decisions are made foster a sense of trust and fairness. Similarly, having a clear path for advancement within the organization, with transparent criteria for promotions and raises, gives employees a reason to stay and grow with the company rather than looking elsewhere for opportunities.

Lastly, the most effective leaders in the restaurant industry recognize the importance of work-life balance, both for themselves and their employees. While the nature of the business often requires long and irregular hours, managers who actively work to create schedules that allow for personal time and who respect their employees' time off contribute significantly to job satisfaction and retention. This might involve implementing rotating schedules for weekend and holiday shifts, being flexible with time-off requests, or even exploring alternative staffing models that provide more predictable hours.

By implementing these leadership and management practices, restaurant owners and managers can significantly reduce turnover rates, create a more positive and productive work environment, and ultimately build a team of dedicated professionals who are committed to the success of the business. The investment in developing these leadership skills pays dividends not just in reduced hiring and training costs, but in improved customer satisfaction, increased profitability, and a reputation as an employer of choice in a competitive industry.

Recap and Actionable Steps

The restaurant industry's notoriously high turnover rate isn't just a statistic; it's a complex challenge that affects every aspect of your business. From the quality of service to your bottom line, the constant churn of staff can feel like trying to bail out a sinking ship with a teaspoon. But here's the truth: it doesn't have to be this way. Throughout this chapter, we've dissected the multifaceted nature of employee retention in the restaurant world, and now it's time to bring it all together with a comprehensive strategy that you can implement starting today.

Employee satisfaction isn't a luxury; it's the bedrock of a thriving restaurant. We've explored how job satisfaction goes far beyond a paycheck, encompassing everything from the work environment to personal growth opportunities. Remember, your staff aren't just cogs in a machine; they're individuals with aspirations, challenges, and the potential to be your greatest asset. By focusing on creating a workplace where people genuinely want to be, you're not just reducing turnover – you're building a team that's invested in your success.

The culture you cultivate within your restaurant's walls can make the difference between a revolving door of employees and a loyal, long-term team. We've discussed the power of fostering an inclusive, supportive environment where every team member feels valued and heard. This isn't about grand gestures; it's about the day-to-day interactions, the policies you implement, and the values you uphold consistently. A positive work culture isn't just good for morale – it's a powerful retention tool that can set your restaurant apart in a competitive industry.

Leadership and management practices are the glue that holds all these elements together. We've examined how effective leadership can dramatically impact turnover rates, exploring best practices that inspire loyalty and drive performance. Remember, great leaders aren't born; they're made through conscious effort, continuous learning, and a genuine commitment to their team's success. By investing in your management skills and those of your supervisory staff, you're creating a ripple effect that touches every aspect of your restaurant's operations.

Now, let's translate these insights into actionable steps you can take to start reducing turnover and building a more stable, successful restaurant operation:

1. Conduct a comprehensive employee satisfaction survey:

• Develop a detailed questionnaire covering all aspects of job satisfaction.

• Ensure anonymity to encourage honest feedback.

• Analyze results to identify key areas for improvement.

• Share findings with your team and involve them in developing solutions.

2. Review and revamp your structure:

• Research current industry standards for all positions.

• Analyze your financial capabilities and project the impact of wage increases.

• Develop a tiered system that rewards longevity and performance.

• Implement a transparent system for raises and promotions.

3. Enhance your benefits package:

• Explore health insurance options, even for part-time staff.

• Consider offering paid time off, even if it's a modest amount to start.

• Implement an employee meal program or increase existing meal benefits.

• Introduce flexible scheduling options where possible.

4. Strengthen your restaurant's culture:

• Define and document your core values and mission statement.

• Create regular team-building activities and social events.

• Establish an employee recognition program to celebrate achievements.

• Implement an open-door policy for management to address concerns. 5. Invest in leadership development:

• Provide management training for all supervisory staff.

• Implement regular performance reviews with two-way feedback.

• Encourage managers to have weekly one-on-one check-ins with team members.

• Create mentorship programs pairing experienced staff with newcomers.

6. Improve onboarding and training processes:

• Develop a structured onboarding program for all new hires.

• Create detailed training manuals for each position.

• Implement a buddy system for new employees' first few weeks.

• Conduct 30, 60, and 90-day check-ins with new hires to address concerns.

7. Establish clear career paths:

• Create and communicate potential career trajectories within your restaurant.

• Offer cross-training opportunities to expand skills and increase engagement.

• Implement a policy of promoting from within whenever possible.

• Provide educational stipends or reimbursement for industry-related courses.

8. Enhance communication channels:

• Hold regular staff meetings to share updates and gather feedback.

• Implement a suggestion box or digital platform for anonymous feedback.

• Create a staff newsletter or bulletin board to keep everyone informed.

• Use scheduling software that allows easy communication between staff and management.

Implementing these strategies isn't a one-time fix; it's an ongoing process of refinement and adaptation. The key is to start somewhere and consistently work towards improvement. Remember, every step you take towards reducing turnover is an investment in your restaurant's future. It's about creating a workplace where people don't just come to earn a paycheck, but where they come to build a career, to be part of something meaningful, and to contribute to a success story they can be proud of.

As you move forward with these actionable steps, keep in mind that change doesn't happen overnight. Be patient with the process and celebrate the small victories along the way. Your commitment to your team's well-being and professional growth will not go unnoticed. In time, you'll find that the energy you invest in retention strategies pays dividends in the form of a more stable, motivated, and high-performing team. This, in turn, translates to better service, happier customers, and a more profitable restaurant. The journey to lower turnover and higher retention starts now, with you taking the lead in creating a restaurant that people are excited to be a part of day in and day out.

Addressing Mental Health in the Restaurant Industry

Problem Introduction

The restaurant industry, with its fast-paced environment and high-pressure situations, has long been a breeding ground for mental health challenges that often go unaddressed, creating a silent epidemic that affects not only the well-being of employees but also the overall health of the businesses they serve. From the relentless demands of customer service to the physical toll of long hours on one's feet, the unique stressors of restaurant work can take a significant toll on the mental health of everyone from line cooks to servers, bartenders to managers, creating a ripple effect that impacts every aspect of operations and ultimately, the bottom line.

These challenges are not isolated incidents but rather systemic issues that permeate the very fabric of the industry, manifesting in various forms such as anxiety, depression, substance abuse, and burnout. The constant pressure to perform at peak levels, often in the face of demanding customers and unpredictable schedules, can leave employees feeling drained, undervalued, and struggling to maintain a sense of balance in their lives. This emotional and psychological strain not only affects individual well-being but also translates into tangible business problems, including high turnover rates, decreased productivity, and a compromised customer experience.

Consider the typical day of a restaurant employee: they might start their shift already exhausted from a late-night closing, only to face a barrage of orders during a busy lunch rush, deal with a difficult customer who leaves them feeling demoralized, and then struggle to find time for a proper meal or moment of rest amidst the chaos. This relentless cycle, repeated day after day, week after week, can wear down even the most resilient individuals, leading to a state of chronic stress that becomes increasingly difficult to manage. The cumulative effect of these experiences can lead to a workforce that is emotionally depleted, physically exhausted, and mentally overwhelmed, creating a perfect storm for mental health issues to take root and flourish.

The significance of addressing mental health in the restaurant industry cannot be overstated, as it directly impacts every facet of business operations. A mentally healthy workforce is more engaged, more productive, and more likely to provide exceptional service that keeps customers coming back. Conversely, employees struggling with mental health issues may find it challenging to maintain the level of enthusiasm and attention to detail that is crucial in the hospitality industry. This can lead to errors in orders, decreased quality of food preparation, and a general decline in the overall dining experience, all of which can have severe consequences for a restaurant's reputation and financial success.

The high turnover rates that plague the industry are often a direct result of the mental health challenges employees face. When workers feel unsupported and overwhelmed, they are more likely to seek employment elsewhere, leading to a constant cycle of hiring and training that drains resources and disrupts team dynamics. This turnover not only represents a significant financial cost in terms of recruitment and training but also erodes the institutional knowledge and cohesive team atmosphere that are essential for a restaurant's smooth operation and success. By addressing mental health concerns head-on, restaurant owners and managers can create a more stable, loyal workforce, reducing turnover costs and fostering a positive work environment that attracts and retains top talent.

The impact of mental health on food safety and hygiene standards is another critical consideration that underscores the importance of addressing this issue. Employees who are struggling with mental health challenges may find it difficult to maintain the high levels of focus and attention to detail required to ensure proper food handling and sanitation practices. This can lead to potentially serious health violations that put both customers and the business at risk. By prioritizing mental health support, restaurants can help ensure that their staff are in the right frame of mind to consistently adhere to safety protocols, protecting both their patrons and their reputation in an industry where a single health violation can have devastating consequences.

Addressing mental health in the restaurant industry is not just a matter of altruism or employee welfare; it's a fundamental business imperative that can make the difference between a thriving establishment and one that struggles to keep its doors open. By creating an environment that supports mental well-being, restaurant owners and managers can unlock the full potential of their staff, fostering a positive atmosphere that translates into better service, higher quality food, and ultimately, a more successful and sustainable business. The challenges are significant, but so too are the rewards for those who recognize the importance of mental health and take proactive steps to support their employees in this crucial area.

Recognizing Signs of Mental Health Issues

I want to start this portion of the book off with this thought… I am not an expert in mental health, am not educated as a mental health professional, or claim to know everything there is to know about the subject. However, having dealt with my own mental health challenges, and through working as an Ambassador for The Burnt Chef Project over the years, I do take pride in trying to understand, and support people in the restaurant industry however I can.

The restaurant industry is a high-pressure environment where the relentless pace, long hours, and constant demands can take a significant toll on the mental well-being of employees at all levels. From the kitchen staff working in sweltering heat to the servers navigating complex customer interactions, the challenges are numerous and often overwhelming. Recognizing the signs of mental health issues in this fast-paced setting is not just a matter of being a good employer; it's a crucial skill that can make the difference between a thriving team and a dysfunctional workplace.

Mental health issues often manifest in subtle ways that can be easily overlooked or misinterpreted in the hustle and bustle of a busy restaurant. A chef who was once the picture of efficiency might start making uncharacteristic mistakes or become irritable with colleagues. A usually cheerful server may begin to withdraw from social interactions or struggle to maintain their usual level of customer service. These changes, while seemingly minor, can be the first indicators of underlying mental health concerns that, if left unaddressed, could escalate into more serious problems affecting both the individual and the entire team.

One of the most common signs of mental health issues in restaurant employees is a noticeable change in their work performance. This could manifest as a decline in the quality of their work, increased absenteeism, or difficulty concentrating on tasks they previously handled with ease. For instance, a line cook who consistently produced perfectly plated dishes might suddenly struggle with presentation or timing. It's essential to approach these situations with empathy and understanding, recognizing that what may appear as a performance issue could be a cry for help.

Emotional volatility is another red flag that managers and colleagues should be attuned to. The restaurant industry is known for its high-stress environment, but when an employee's emotional responses become disproportionate to the situation at hand, it may indicate underlying mental health concerns. This could manifest as sudden outbursts of anger, unexplained bouts of tearfulness, or extreme mood swings that disrupt the harmony of the team. In an industry where teamwork is paramount, these emotional fluctuations can have a ripple effect, impacting not only the individual but also their colleagues and potentially even the dining experience of customers.

Physical symptoms can also be indicators of mental health issues. Chronic fatigue, unexplained aches and pains, or frequent complaints of illness might be physical manifestations of psychological distress. In a job that demands physical stamina, these symptoms can be particularly debilitating. A server who once effortlessly navigated a busy dining room might start to appear visibly exhausted or struggle with the physical demands of the job. It's crucial to recognize that these physical symptoms may be interconnected with mental health and not dismiss them as mere laziness or incompetence.

Changes in social behavior are often telltale signs of mental health struggles. An employee who was once the life of the staff room might start isolating themselves, avoiding social interactions, or declining invitations to after-work gatherings. Conversely, someone might exhibit uncharacteristically risky or impulsive behavior, such as increased alcohol consumption during staff outings or engaging in conflicts with colleagues. These social changes can be particularly noticeable in the close-knit environment of a restaurant, where team dynamics play a crucial role in the smooth operation of the establishment.

To effectively recognize these signs, management must be trained in mental health awareness. This training should go beyond simply identifying symptoms; it should equip managers with the tools to approach these situations with sensitivity and professionalism. Role-playing exercises can be invaluable in preparing managers for difficult conversations. For example, practicing how to address a bartender who has been making more mistakes than usual or a hostess who seems withdrawn and disengaged can help managers feel more confident in these delicate situations.

Implementing a system for regular check-ins with employees can create opportunities to spot mental health issues early. These check-ins should be more than just performance reviews; they should be genuine conversations about an employee's well-being, challenges, and aspirations. By fostering an environment where employees feel comfortable discussing their mental health, managers can catch potential issues before they escalate. This proactive approach not only benefits the individual employee but also contributes to a more stable and productive work environment.

It's crucial to emphasize that recognizing signs of mental health issues is not about diagnosing employees or playing the role of a therapist. Instead, it's about creating a supportive environment where mental health is taken seriously and employees feel valued as whole individuals, not just as workers. This approach can lead to earlier interventions, whether that means adjusting work schedules, providing resources for professional help, or simply offering a listening ear. By prioritizing mental health awareness, restaurant managers can create a more resilient, loyal, and high-performing team, ultimately benefiting both the employees and the business as a whole.

Support Systems and Resources

The restaurant industry is notorious for its high-pressure environment, long hours, and demanding physical and emotional labor. These factors can take a significant toll on the mental health of employees at all levels, from dishwashers to executive chefs. Establishing robust support systems within the workplace is not just a nice-to-have; it's a critical component of running a successful and sustainable restaurant business. When employees feel supported and have access to resources that can help them navigate their mental health challenges, they're more likely to perform better, stay longer, and contribute positively to the overall work atmosphere.

Creating an effective support system starts with acknowledging that mental health is as important as physical health. This mindset shift is crucial for restaurant owners and managers who want to foster a healthier work environment. It's about recognizing that investing in your staff's mental well-being is not just a moral imperative but also a sound business decision. Happy, mentally healthy employees are more productive, creative, and resilient in the face of the daily challenges that come with working in a fast-paced restaurant setting.

One of the most impactful ways to support your staff's mental health is by implementing an Employee Assistance Program (EAP). An EAP is a confidential counseling service that provides employees with access to professional mental health support at no cost to them. This can include short-term counseling sessions, referrals to long-term therapy, and resources for dealing with personal issues that may be affecting their work performance. The beauty of an EAP is that it offers a safe, confidential space for employees to address their concerns without fear of judgment or repercussions in the workplace.

The Burnt Chef Project is one of the leading platforms that I always recommend to anyone interested in providing better support for the people. I personally act as an ambassador for them and have seen the value that they provide to our industry firsthand.

Another valuable resource to consider is mental health first aid training for managers and supervisors. This type of training equips leadership with the skills to recognize signs of mental distress in their team members and provides them with strategies to offer initial support and guide individuals towards appropriate professional help. By investing in this training, you're not only building a more compassionate leadership team but also creating a first line of defense in identifying and addressing mental health issues before they escalate.

Implementing a peer support program can also be incredibly effective in the restaurant setting. This involves training select employees to act as mental health ambassadors within the workplace. These individuals can serve as a bridge between staff and management, offering a listening ear and directing colleagues to appropriate resources when needed. The peer support model works particularly well in the restaurant industry because it leverages the camaraderie that often develops among staff members who work closely together in high-stress situations.

Creating dedicated spaces for relaxation and decompression within the restaurant can also significantly impact employee mental health. While space is often at a premium in restaurants, even a small, quiet area where staff can take a few minutes to breathe and reset during a hectic shift can make a world of difference. This space could be as simple as a converted storage room with comfortable seating, calming decor, and perhaps resources like mindfulness apps or stress-relief tools.

Flexibility in scheduling, where possible, can also serve as a powerful mental health resource. While the nature of restaurant work often requires set schedules, finding ways to accommodate employee needs can significantly reduce stress. This might mean implementing a system for shift swaps, offering longer breaks between double shifts, or even exploring alternative scheduling models like four-day workweeks for certain positions. The key is to demonstrate that you value your employees' time and understand their need for work-life balance.

Remember that implementing these resources is just the first step. Regularly promoting their availability and normalizing their use is crucial for their effectiveness. Consider incorporating mental health check-ins into your regular staff meetings, displaying information about available resources prominently in staff areas, and leading by example by openly discussing mental health and self-care practices. By consistently reinforcing the importance of mental health and the resources available, you create a culture where seeking support is seen as a strength rather than a weakness.

Ultimately, the goal of establishing these support systems and resources is to create a work environment where employees feel valued, supported, and equipped to handle the unique challenges of the restaurant industry. By investing in your staff's mental well-being, you're not just improving their individual lives; you're building a more resilient, loyal, and high-performing team that can weather the storms of this demanding industry and contribute to the long-term success of your restaurant.

Creating a Dialogue Around Mental Health

The restaurant industry has long been characterized by its fast-paced, high-pressure environment, where the focus on customer satisfaction and operational efficiency often overshadows the well-being of those working behind the scenes. This intense atmosphere, coupled with long hours, irregular schedules, and the constant demand for perfection, can take a significant toll on the mental health of restaurant employees at all levels, from dishwashers and line cooks to servers and management. The time has come for a fundamental shift in how we approach mental health within our industry, moving beyond the outdated notion that stress and burnout are simply part of the job description and towards a more compassionate, supportive, and open dialogue that acknowledges the importance of mental well-being in creating a thriving workplace.

Initiating conversations about mental health in the restaurant setting requires a delicate balance of sensitivity, authenticity, and practical action. It's not enough to simply pay lip service to the idea of mental health support; restaurant owners and managers must actively work to create an environment where employees feel safe and comfortable discussing their struggles without fear of judgment or repercussion. This process begins with leadership setting the tone by openly acknowledging the challenges inherent in the industry and demonstrating a genuine commitment to addressing them. By sharing personal experiences or struggles with mental health, those in positions of authority can help normalize these conversations and break down the barriers that often prevent employees from seeking help or support when they need it most.

One effective strategy for fostering open dialogue is to incorporate regular check-ins or team meetings specifically dedicated to discussing mental health and well-being. These sessions should be structured in a way that encourages participation from all staff members, regardless of their position within the restaurant hierarchy. Consider implementing a rotating system where different team members are responsible for leading these discussions, allowing for a diversity of perspectives and experiences to be shared. During these meetings, it's crucial to create a non-judgmental space where employees feel empowered to voice their concerns, share coping strategies, and offer support to their colleagues. This collaborative approach not only helps to reduce the stigma surrounding mental health issues but also strengthens team bonds and fosters a sense of community within the workplace.

To further support these efforts, restaurant owners and managers should consider bringing in mental health professionals or experts to conduct workshops or training sessions for staff. These sessions can provide valuable information on recognizing signs of mental health issues, developing coping mechanisms, and understanding how to support colleagues who may be struggling. By investing in this type of education, restaurants demonstrate a commitment to their employees' well-being while also equipping staff with the tools they need to navigate the unique challenges of the industry. Additionally, these workshops can serve as a springboard for ongoing conversations and initiatives around mental health, helping to integrate these important discussions into the fabric of daily operations.

Another crucial aspect of creating a dialogue around mental health is ensuring that employees have access to resources and support systems both within and outside of the workplace. This might include establishing partnerships with local mental health organizations like The Burnt Chef Project, providing information on counseling services or support groups, or even offering on-site counseling sessions for staff. By making these resources readily available and actively promoting their use, restaurants can demonstrate a tangible commitment to supporting their employees' mental health. It's important to remember that different individuals may have different needs or preferences when it comes to seeking support, so offering a variety of options can help ensure that all employees feel comfortable accessing the help they need.

In addition to formal support systems, fostering peer-to-peer support networks within the restaurant can be incredibly powerful in creating a culture of openness and understanding around mental health. Encourage employees to look out for one another, to check in with colleagues who may be struggling, and to offer support or a listening ear when needed. This might involve implementing a buddy system, where employees are paired up to provide mutual support, or creating designated "safe spaces" within the restaurant where staff can take a moment to decompress or have private conversations. By empowering employees to support one another, restaurants can create a more resilient and compassionate workplace culture that is better equipped to handle the unique stressors of the industry.

As we work to create a more open dialogue around mental health in the restaurant industry, it's essential to recognize that this is an ongoing process that requires consistent effort and attention. Regular evaluation and adjustment of mental health initiatives are crucial to ensuring their effectiveness and relevance. Solicit feedback from employees on what's working well and what could be improved and be willing to adapt your approach based on this input. Remember that creating lasting change in workplace culture takes time, patience, and a willingness to learn and grow together as a team. By maintaining a commitment to open communication and continuous improvement, restaurants can create an environment where mental health is prioritized, stigma is reduced, and employees feel truly supported in all aspects of their well-being.

Work-Life Balance

The restaurant industry is notorious for its demanding schedules, long hours, and high-stress environments. These factors can take a significant toll on the mental and physical well-being of employees, from servers and kitchen staff to managers and owners. Achieving a healthy work-life balance is not just a luxury; it's a necessity for maintaining a productive, motivated, and stable workforce. In an industry where burnout is all too common, implementing strategies to improve work-life balance can be a game-changer for both individual employees and the overall success of the restaurant.

One of the most impactful strategies for improving work-life balance is implementing flexible scheduling. This doesn't mean throwing structure out the window, but rather creating a system that allows employees to have more control over their work hours. Consider using scheduling software that allows staff to input their availability and preferences. This not only helps ensure that shifts are covered but also gives employees the ability to plan their personal lives around work commitments. Additionally, offering split shifts or shorter workdays can provide more opportunities for staff to attend to personal matters, pursue hobbies, or simply rest and recharge.

Another crucial aspect of work-life balance is setting clear boundaries between work and personal time. In the age of constant connectivity, it's easy for work to bleed into personal hours, especially for management. Establish a policy that discourages after-hours communication unless it's an absolute emergency. This means no late-night texts about shift changes or early morning emails about inventory. By respecting these boundaries, you're showing your staff that you value their personal time and understand the importance of disconnecting from work. This respect often translates into increased loyalty and job satisfaction, which can significantly reduce turnover rates.

Encouraging and facilitating time off is another vital component of fostering work-life balance. Many restaurant employees, particularly those in lower-wage positions, may feel pressure to work as many hours as possible or fear taking time off will jeopardize their job security. Create a culture that not only allows but encourages employees to use their vacation days. Consider implementing a minimum number of days off per month or quarter to ensure everyone is getting necessary rest. For those in management positions, lead by example. When managers and owners take time off, it sends a powerful message that it's okay for everyone to do so. Nobody should ever feel guilty for taking time off.

Promoting physical and mental wellness activities can also contribute significantly to improved work-life balance. Consider partnering with local gyms or wellness centers to offer discounted memberships to your staff. Organize group activities like yoga classes or meditation sessions that employees can participate in before or after shifts. These initiatives not only contribute to better physical health but also provide opportunities for team bonding outside of the work environment. Remember, a staff that exercises together and takes care of their mental health together is likely to work more cohesively and efficiently during busy service hours.

Professional development and career growth opportunities are often overlooked aspects of work-life balance, but they play a crucial role in employee satisfaction and retention. Offer training sessions, workshops, or even tuition assistance for courses related to the restaurant industry. This not only helps employees develop new skills and advance their careers but also shows that you're invested in their long-term success. When staff members feel they're growing professionally, they're more likely to find fulfillment in their work, which positively impacts their overall life satisfaction.

Creating a supportive work environment that acknowledges the challenges of maintaining work-life balance is essential. Regular check-ins with staff about their workload and stress levels can help identify potential issues before they become major problems. Consider implementing an open-door policy where employees feel comfortable discussing their concerns about work-life balance. Sometimes, simple adjustments like reassigning tasks or providing additional support during peak hours can make a significant difference in an employee's ability to manage their work and personal life effectively.

The impact of improved work-life balance on mental well-being and productivity cannot be overstated. When employees have the time and energy to pursue personal interests, spend time with family and friends, and take care of their physical and mental health, they bring a renewed sense of energy and focus to their work. This translates into better customer service, increased efficiency, and a more positive work atmosphere. Staff members who feel their personal lives are respected and supported are more likely to go above and beyond in their roles, contributing to the overall success of the restaurant.

Implementing these strategies requires a commitment from all levels of management and may necessitate some initial adjustments to operations. However, the long-term benefits far outweigh any short-term challenges. Restaurants that prioritize work-life balance often see reduced turnover rates, which can save thousands of dollars in hiring and training costs. They also benefit from improved employee morale, which can lead to better teamwork, increased creativity in problem-solving, and a more positive dining experience for customers. In an industry where margins are tight and competition is fierce, creating a workplace that values and supports work-life balance can be a significant differentiator in attracting and retaining top talent.

Recap and Actionable Steps

Mental health in the restaurant industry is a complex issue that demands our immediate attention and action. The fast-paced, high-stress environment of kitchens and dining rooms can take a significant toll on the well-being of staff members, from line cooks to servers, and even management. It's crucial to recognize that addressing mental health isn't just about being a compassionate employer – it's a strategic move that can dramatically improve your restaurant's performance, reduce turnover, and create a more positive workplace culture that benefits everyone involved.

Throughout this chapter, we've explored various aspects of mental health in the restaurant setting, from recognizing the signs of distress to implementing support systems and fostering open dialogues. We've discussed the importance of work-life balance and how it contributes to overall mental well-being. Now, it's time to consolidate these insights into a comprehensive strategy that you can implement in your establishment. By taking proactive steps to support your staff's mental health, you're not only investing in their well-being but also in the long-term success of your business.

Let's recap the key strategies we've covered and break them down into actionable steps you can start implementing today. Remember, change doesn't happen overnight, but with consistent effort and a genuine commitment to improvement, you can create a workplace that supports mental health and helps your team thrive. These steps are designed to be practical and adaptable to various restaurant settings, whether you're running a small family-owned diner or managing a large upscale establishment.

Here's a step-by-step guide to fostering a mentally healthier work environment in your restaurant:

• Conduct a mental health audit of your workplace: - Assess current stress levels among staff - Identify potential triggers or stressors in the work environment - Review existing policies and procedures that may impact mental health - Gather anonymous feedback from employees about their mental health concerns • Implement a mental health training program for management: - Schedule regular workshops on recognizing signs of mental health issues - Provide resources for managers to learn about mental health first aid - Train leaders in empathetic communication and active listening skills - Establish clear protocols for addressing mental health concerns • Create a comprehensive mental health resource guide: - Compile a list of local mental health professionals and support groups - Include information on employee assistance programs like The Burnt Chef Project. - Add crisis hotline numbers and online resources for immediate support - Distribute the guide to all employees and make it easily accessible • Establish a peer support system: - Train volunteer employees to become mental health ambassadors - Set up a buddy system for new hires to help them acclimate - Create safe spaces for staff to decompress during shifts - Encourage regular check-ins between team members • Revamp scheduling practices to promote work-life balance: - Implement a fair and transparent shift allocation system - Ensure adequate staffing to prevent burnout - Offer flexible scheduling options when possible - Respect time off and discourage off-hours work communications • Develop a mental health-friendly company culture: - Lead by example in prioritizing mental health - Regularly discuss mental well-being in team meetings - Celebrate mental health awareness days and months - Encourage breaks and time for self-care during shifts • Implement stress-reduction initiatives: - Introduce pre-shift mindfulness or meditation sessions - Offer on-site yoga or exercise classes - Create a quiet room for staff to use during breaks - Provide healthy snacks and hydration stations • Establish clear communication channels: - Set up an anonymous suggestion box for mental health concerns - Hold regular one-on-one check-ins between managers and staff - Create an open-door policy for discussing mental health issues - Use team meetings to address collective stress and find solutions • Review and improve workplace policies: - Ensure sick leave policies include mental health days - Implement a zero-tolerance policy for workplace bullying or harassment - Create guidelines for addressing conflicts and grievances -

Develop a return-to-work program for employees recovering from mental health issues • Measure and monitor progress: - Conduct regular surveys to assess employee well-being - Track key metrics like turnover rates and absenteeism - Gather feedback on the effectiveness of mental health initiatives - Adjust strategies based on results and employee input

Implementing these steps will require time, effort, and resources, but the payoff in terms of employee satisfaction, productivity, and retention will be substantial. Start by prioritizing a few key areas that you feel will have the most immediate impact in your specific restaurant environment. As you begin to see positive changes, you can gradually expand your mental health initiatives.

Remember, creating a mentally healthy workplace is an ongoing process. It requires constant attention, adaptation, and a willingness to listen to your staff's needs. By making mental health a priority, you're not just improving the lives of your employees – you're also setting your restaurant up for long-term success in an industry known for its challenges. Your commitment to mental health can become a powerful differentiator, attracting top talent and fostering loyalty among both staff and customers.

As you embark on this journey to improve mental health in your restaurant, keep in mind that small changes can lead to significant results. Every step you take towards supporting your team's mental well-being is a step towards a more resilient, productive, and harmonious workplace. The restaurant industry has long been overdue for a mental health revolution, and by taking action now, you're positioning yourself at the forefront of this crucial movement.

Boosting Profitability Through Strategic Management

Problem Introduction

The restaurant industry has always been a challenging landscape, but recent economic shifts have made maintaining profitability more difficult than ever before. Rising food costs, increasing labor expenses, and unpredictable consumer spending habits have created a perfect storm of financial pressure for restaurant owners and managers. These challenges are not just temporary hurdles; they represent a fundamental shift in the industry that requires a new approach to business management.

In this evolving economic climate, the difference between a thriving restaurant and one that's barely staying afloat often comes down to the implementation of strategic management practices. Strategic management isn't just a buzzword; it's a comprehensive approach to running your business that can make the difference between success and failure in today's competitive market. It involves analyzing every aspect of your operation, from menu pricing to staff scheduling, and making data-driven decisions to optimize your profitability.

Consider the impact of even small inefficiencies when magnified across the thousands of transactions your restaurant processes each month. A slight miscalculation in portion sizes, an inefficient kitchen layout, or overstaffing during slow periods can eat away at your profit margins, turning what should be a profitable shift into a financial loss. These seemingly minor issues, when left unaddressed, compound over time and can seriously threaten the long-term viability of your business.

The importance of strategic management in overcoming these challenges cannot be overstated. It provides a framework for identifying and addressing inefficiencies, maximizing resource utilization, and adapting to market changes quickly and effectively. By adopting a strategic approach, you're not just reacting to problems as they arise; you're proactively shaping the future of your business. This means anticipating trends, understanding your customer base deeply, and constantly refining your operations to stay ahead of the competition.

One of the most critical aspects of strategic management in the restaurant industry is the ability to balance quality and cost. It's not simply about cutting expenses across the board; it's about making intelligent decisions that maintain or even enhance the customer experience while improving your bottom line. This might involve renegotiating contracts with suppliers, redesigning your menu to focus on high-margin items, or investing in technology that streamlines operations and reduces labor costs.

Also, strategic management extends beyond the day-to-day operations of your restaurant. It encompasses long-term planning, brand positioning, and market analysis. In an industry where consumer preferences can shift rapidly, having a clear, adaptable strategy is essential. This might involve diversifying your offerings, exploring new revenue streams like catering or meal kits, or repositioning your brand to appeal to a changing demographic.

The implementation of strategic management practices can seem daunting, especially if you're used to running your restaurant based on instinct and experience alone. However, the benefits far outweigh the initial challenges of adopting this approach. Restaurants that embrace strategic management often see improvements not just in their profitability, but in customer satisfaction, employee retention, and overall operational efficiency. It's about creating a sustainable business model that can weather economic uncertainties and position your restaurant for long-term success.

As we go deeper into the specific strategies and techniques for boosting profitability, keep in mind that the goal is to create a resilient, adaptable business that can thrive in any economic climate. The challenges facing the restaurant industry are significant, but they're not insurmountable. With the right approach to strategic management, you can transform these challenges into opportunities for growth and innovation, setting your restaurant apart in a crowded and competitive market.

Optimizing Menu for Higher Margins

In the restaurant industry, where profit margins are notoriously slim and competition is fierce, menu optimization stands as a powerful tool for boosting profitability. This process, often referred to as menu engineering, involves a strategic approach to designing and pricing your menu items to maximize revenue while ensuring customer satisfaction. It's a delicate balance that requires a deep understanding of your costs, your clientele, and the psychology of consumer behavior.

At its core, menu engineering is about analyzing the performance of each dish on your menu. This analysis goes beyond simply looking at which items sell the most; it involves a comprehensive examination of each dish's popularity and profitability. By categorizing menu items based on these two factors, you can make informed decisions about which dishes to promote, which to redesign, and which to potentially remove from your menu altogether.

The first step in this process is to calculate the food cost percentage for each item on your menu. This involves determining the exact cost of ingredients for each dish and comparing it to the selling price. While many in the industry suggest aiming for a food cost percentage between 28% and 35%, it's crucial to remember that this can vary depending on your restaurant's concept and location. High-end establishments might have lower food cost percentages due to higher menu prices, while quick-service restaurants might operate with slightly higher percentages. Always remember that the dollar contribution of any given item is more important than the cost %. Would you not rather sell a 40% cost item that makes you $15 every time you sell one, than a 25% cost item that makes you $8. At the end of the day, we are in the business of making money, not percentage.

Once you've calculated your food costs, the next step is to analyze the popularity of each dish. This information can typically be found in your point-of-sale system, which tracks the number of each item sold over a given period. By combining this data with your profitability analysis, you can categorize your menu items into four groups: stars (high profitability, high popularity), plow horses (low profitability, high popularity), puzzles (high profitability, low popularity), and dogs (low profitability, low popularity).

Stars are your menu's superstars - these are the items you want to prominently feature. They're not only popular with your customers but also contribute significantly to your bottom line. Consider placing these items in the 'golden triangle' of your menu - the area where customers' eyes naturally gravitate first, typically the upper right corner. You might also create a special section highlighting these dishes or train your staff to recommend them to indecisive diners.

Plow horses, while popular, aren't contributing as much to your profits. However, their popularity suggests that customers enjoy them, so removing them isn't necessarily the answer. Instead, look for ways to increase their profitability. This might involve tweaking the recipe to reduce ingredient costs, slightly increasing the price, or pairing them with high-margin side dishes or beverages.

Puzzles present an interesting challenge. These dishes are profitable but aren't selling as well as they could be. The solution often lies in marketing. Consider renaming the dish to make it more appealing, improving its description on the menu, or having your servers promote it more actively. Sometimes, simply moving the item to a more prominent position on the menu can increase its visibility and, consequently, its sales.

Dogs are the items that are neither profitable nor popular. While it might be tempting to immediately remove these from your menu, it's worth considering why they're there in the first place. Does the dish cater to a specific dietary requirement? Is it a longtime favorite of a few loyal customers? If there's no compelling reason to keep it, consider replacing it with a new dish that has the potential to become a star or a plow horse.

Beyond categorization, the design and layout of your menu play a crucial role in guiding customers' choices. Studies have shown that diners tend to remember the first and last items in each menu category more than those in the middle. Use this knowledge to your advantage by placing your most profitable items in these prime positions. Additionally, consider using visual cues like boxes or different fonts to draw attention to high-margin dishes.

The language used in your menu descriptions can significantly impact sales. Vivid, sensory-rich descriptions can make dishes more appealing and can even influence how customers perceive the taste of the food. Instead of simply listing ingredients, paint a picture with your words. For example, instead of "Grilled Chicken with Vegetables," try "Herb-Marinated Chicken Breast, Flame-Grilled to Perfection, Served with a Medley of Seasonal Roasted Vegetables."

Pricing strategy is another crucial aspect of menu engineering. While it might be tempting to use round numbers, research has shown that prices ending in .25 or .50 are often perceived as better value than round numbers. However, for high-end restaurants, round numbers might be more appropriate as they can convey a sense of quality and precision.

It's also worth considering the psychology of price anchoring. By including a few high-priced items on your menu, you can make other items seem more reasonably priced in comparison. This doesn't mean adding outrageously expensive dishes that won't sell; rather, it's about strategically placing premium items that some customers will order, while others will use as a reference point for the rest of the menu.

Remember, menu engineering is not a one-time task but an ongoing process. Consumer preferences change, ingredient costs fluctuate, and new food trends emerge. Regularly analyzing your menu's performance and making adjustments accordingly is crucial for maintaining and improving your restaurant's profitability. Consider reviewing your menu quarterly, or at minimum, annually.

By applying these menu engineering techniques, you can significantly boost your restaurant's profitability. However, it's important to balance these strategies with maintaining the integrity of your restaurant's concept and the quality of your offerings. The goal is not just to increase profits in the short term, but to create a sustainable business model that keeps customers coming back for more.

Effective Cost Management

In the high-stakes world of restaurant management, where profit margins can be incredibly thin, mastering the art of effective cost management is not just a skill—it's a survival strategy. The restaurant industry is notoriously challenging, with unexpected expenses lurking around every corner and the constant pressure to deliver exceptional experiences while keeping costs in check. It's a delicate balance that requires a keen eye for detail, a strategic mindset, and the willingness to make tough decisions when necessary. For those who have spent countless hours in the hustle and bustle of a busy kitchen or the controlled chaos of a packed dining room, the importance of managing costs effectively is all too familiar.

At its core, effective cost management in restaurants is about identifying and eliminating unnecessary expenditures without compromising the quality of food or service that keeps customers coming back. This process begins with a thorough examination of every aspect of your operation, from the ingredients used in your signature dishes to the energy consumption of your kitchen equipment. It's about questioning every expense and asking yourself, "Is this truly essential to our success?" Sometimes, the answers might surprise you. That fancy imported cheese that you thought was elevating your pizza might actually be eating into your profits without significantly enhancing the customer experience. Or perhaps that state-of-the-art espresso machine, while impressive, is overkill for your casual café and a more modest model would suffice.

One of the most effective tools in the cost management arsenal is a comprehensive inventory management system. There are so many on the market to choose from, and it can be hard to know which way to go. I always recommend Margin Edge to anyone I speak with, and it is what we use every day in our restaurant.

This process goes beyond simply counting bottles and cans at the end of the night. A robust inventory system tracks the movement of every ingredient, from the moment it enters your establishment to when it's served to a customer. By implementing such a system, you can identify waste, prevent over-ordering, and even catch potential theft. For example, let's say you notice that your high-end vodka usage doesn't align with sales figures. This could indicate several issues: bartenders over-pouring, inaccurate recipe measurements, or even employee theft. Armed with this information, you can take targeted action to address the problem, whether it's retraining staff, adjusting recipes, or implementing stricter controls.

Another critical aspect of cost management is labor optimization. Labor costs often represent the largest expense for restaurants, and finding ways to maximize efficiency without sacrificing quality is crucial. This doesn't mean cutting staff indiscriminately or overworking your team. Instead, it's about smart scheduling, cross-training employees to handle multiple roles, and leveraging technology to streamline operations. Consider implementing a system that integrates with your scheduling software. This allows you to analyze sales data alongside labor costs, helping you identify peak hours and adjust staffing accordingly. You might discover that you're overstaffed during what you thought were busy periods, or that you could benefit from an extra set of hands during unexpected rushes.

We use Hatch Insights to support us through this process. There is always so much data to look at, and understanding what to act on next can be a challenge. Hatch definitely makes that easier for our teams by providing insights in one minute, without having to click through a bunch of dashboards.

Energy costs are another area where significant savings can be found with a bit of strategic thinking. The kitchen is often the biggest energy consumer in a restaurant, with ovens, refrigerators, and dishwashers running constantly. Investing in energy-efficient appliances might seem like a large upfront cost, but the long-term savings can be substantial. Additionally, simple changes like installing LED lighting, using low-flow faucets, and implementing a startup/shutdown schedule for equipment can lead to noticeable reductions in utility bills. Some restaurants have even found success in redesigning their kitchens to be more energy-efficient, creating workflows that minimize the distance between stations and reduce the need for energy-intensive equipment to be running constantly.

Vendor negotiations and supply chain management are often overlooked aspects of cost control, but they can have a significant impact on your bottom line. Developing strong relationships with your suppliers can lead to better prices, more favorable payment terms, and even exclusive access to high-quality ingredients. Don't be afraid to shop around and compare prices regularly. However, remember that the lowest price isn't always the best deal. Consider factors like quality, reliability, and flexibility when choosing suppliers. Sometimes, paying a bit more for a vendor who can deliver consistently high-quality products or who's willing to work with you during busy periods can be worth the extra cost in terms of customer satisfaction and operational stability.

One often underutilized tool in the cost management toolkit is data analysis. In today's digital age, restaurants have access to an unprecedented amount of data about their operations, customers, and market trends. Leveraging this data can provide invaluable insights into where your money is going and where you might be able to cut costs. For instance, analyzing sales data might reveal that certain menu items are consistently unpopular or have low profit margins. This information can guide menu engineering decisions, helping you focus on high-profit, popular items and eliminate or revamp underperforming dishes. Similarly, customer feedback data can help you identify areas where you might be overspending on features or services that customers don't value, allowing you to reallocate those resources more effectively.

Implementing effective cost management strategies requires a commitment from everyone in the organization, from the head chef to the dishwasher. It's crucial to foster a culture of cost-consciousness without creating an atmosphere of penny-pinching that could negatively impact morale or customer experience. Educate your staff about the importance of cost control and how it relates to the overall success of the business. Encourage them to come up with ideas for reducing waste or improving efficiency. Sometimes, the best cost-saving ideas come from the employees who are on the front lines every day. By involving your team in the process, you not only gain valuable insights but also create a sense of ownership and pride in the restaurant's financial health.

Remember, effective cost management is not a one-time effort but an ongoing process of evaluation, adjustment, and innovation. The restaurant industry is constantly evolving, and what works today might not be as effective tomorrow. Stay informed about industry trends, new technologies, and changing customer preferences. Be willing to experiment with new approaches and learn from both successes and failures. By maintaining a proactive and flexible approach to cost management, you can navigate the challenges of the restaurant industry and build a more resilient, profitable business that stands the test of time.

Leveraging Technology for Efficiency

In the fast-paced world of restaurants, where every second counts and every dollar matters, technology has emerged as a game-changer for those willing to embrace it. The integration of cutting-edge solutions into daily operations isn't just about keeping up with the times; it's about revolutionizing the way we approach efficiency, customer service, and ultimately, profitability. From streamlined ordering processes to data-driven decision making, the right technological tools can transform a struggling establishment into a well-oiled machine, capable of navigating the choppy waters of the food service industry with newfound agility and precision.

At the heart of this technological revolution lies the Point of Sale (POS) system, a cornerstone of modern restaurant management that has evolved far beyond its humble origins as a simple cash register. Today's POS systems are sophisticated hubs of information and control, offering a wealth of features that can dramatically improve operational efficiency. These systems seamlessly integrate various aspects of restaurant management, from order taking and inventory tracking to employee scheduling and customer relationship management, all within a single, user-friendly interface that can be accessed from anywhere, at any time.

The benefits of implementing a modern POS system are manifold and can have a profound impact on a restaurant's bottom line. For starters, these systems significantly reduce the likelihood of human error in order taking and processing, ensuring that customers receive exactly what they ordered and minimizing costly mistakes that can lead to wasted food and dissatisfied diners. The speed at which orders can be processed and transmitted to the kitchen means faster table turnover, allowing restaurants to serve more customers during peak hours without sacrificing quality or service.

But the advantages of a robust POS system extend far beyond the dining room floor. The wealth of data these systems collect and analyze can provide invaluable insights into every aspect of a restaurant's operations. By meticulously tracking sales patterns, inventory levels, and labor costs, restaurant owners and managers can make informed decisions about menu offerings, staffing levels, and pricing strategies. This data-driven approach to management can help identify underperforming menu items, optimize inventory to reduce waste, and ensure that staffing levels are perfectly aligned with customer demand, all of which contribute to improved profitability.

Complementing the POS system, management software designed specifically for the restaurant industry can further enhance operational efficiency and streamline administrative tasks. These powerful tools can automate many time-consuming processes, such as employee scheduling, payroll management, and inventory ordering. By reducing the administrative burden on managers and owners, this software frees up valuable time that can be redirected towards more strategic initiatives, such as menu development, staff training, and marketing efforts.

The implementation of these technological solutions, however, is not without its challenges. The initial investment can be substantial, and there's often a learning curve associated with adopting new systems. It's crucial to choose solutions that are not only powerful but also intuitive and user-friendly, ensuring that staff at all levels can quickly adapt to the new technology. Additionally, proper training and ongoing support are essential to maximize the benefits of these systems and minimize disruptions during the transition period.

Despite these potential hurdles, the long-term benefits of leveraging technology for efficiency in the restaurant industry are undeniable. Restaurants that embrace these solutions often find themselves better equipped to handle the myriad challenges of the modern food service landscape, from fluctuating food costs to changing consumer preferences. By automating routine tasks, providing real-time insights, and enabling data-driven decision making, technology empowers restaurant owners and managers to focus on what truly matters: delivering exceptional dining experiences and building lasting relationships with customers.

As we look to the future, it's clear that technology will continue to play an increasingly important role in shaping the restaurant industry.

From artificial intelligence-powered inventory management to augmented reality menu presentations, the possibilities are endless. Those who stay ahead of the curve, continuously exploring and adopting new technological solutions, will be best positioned to thrive in an ever-evolving marketplace. The key is to approach technology not as a replacement for human touch and creativity, but as a powerful tool that enhances and amplifies the unique qualities that make a restaurant truly special. My general rule of thumb for technology is this... If it is not reducing the time it takes to perform a task, or driving guest count and revenue, it may be hard to justify the cost. However, every restaurant is different and only you will truly know the answer.

Employee Productivity and Business Outcomes

In the fast-paced world of restaurants, where every second counts and every dollar matters, the link between employee productivity and profitability is not just a theory—it's a fundamental reality that can make or break your business. Surprisingly, although several restaurants measure units of productivity, and almost all of them measure labor costs, few actually understand the importance of understanding how the two work together.

The bustling kitchen, the attentive servers, and the meticulous management team all play crucial roles in crafting the dining experience that keeps customers coming back and, ultimately, determines your bottom line. Understanding and optimizing this connection is essential for restaurant owners and managers who want to thrive in an industry known for its razor-thin margins and high-pressure environment.

At its core, employee productivity in the restaurant setting is about maximizing output while minimizing wasted time and resources. It's the server who effortlessly manages multiple tables, ensuring each guest feels attended to without a single order missed. It's the line cook who executes dishes with precision and speed, maintaining quality even during the busiest rush. It's the manager who orchestrates the entire operation, making real-time decisions that keep the restaurant running like a well-oiled machine. When these elements align, the result is a seamless dining experience that not only satisfies customers but also optimizes labor costs and enhances overall profitability.

To truly grasp the impact of employee productivity on your restaurant's success, it's crucial to establish clear metrics and consistently measure performance. Start by tracking key performance indicators (KPIs) that directly relate to productivity and profitability. These might include sales per labor hour, which measures how much revenue is generated for each hour of work; Covers per labor hour, which measures how many people are required to serve the number of guests visiting the restaurant; table turn time, which indicates how efficiently your staff manages seating and service; and food cost percentage, which reflects how well your kitchen staff controls portions and minimizes waste. By regularly monitoring these metrics, you can identify trends, spot areas for improvement, and make data-driven decisions to boost productivity across your entire operation.

Implementing a robust training program is one of the most effective ways to improve employee productivity and, consequently, your restaurant's profitability. This goes beyond the basic onboarding process—it should be an ongoing commitment to developing your staff's skills and knowledge. Consider creating a comprehensive training manual that covers everything from proper food handling techniques to advanced customer service strategies. Regularly scheduled training sessions can keep your team updated on menu changes, upselling techniques, and efficiency-boosting practices. Remember, a well-trained employee is not only more productive but also more confident and satisfied in their role, which can significantly reduce turnover—a persistent challenge in the restaurant industry that directly impacts your bottom line.

Technology can be a game-changer when it comes to enhancing employee productivity and streamlining operations. Investing in a modern point-of-sale (POS) system can dramatically reduce order errors, speed up service, and provide valuable data on sales patterns and inventory management. Mobile ordering tablets for servers can eliminate the need for them to run back and forth to a stationary terminal, allowing them to spend more time interacting with guests and potentially increasing sales through suggestive selling. In the kitchen, digital display systems can improve communication between front and back of house, ensuring orders are prepared accurately and efficiently. While the initial investment in such technologies may seem daunting, the long-term benefits in terms of increased productivity and profitability can be substantial.

Creating a positive work environment is another crucial factor in boosting employee productivity and, by extension, your restaurant's profitability. This goes beyond simply offering competitive wages. Focus on fostering a culture of respect, recognition, and growth opportunities. Implement an employee recognition program that rewards exceptional performance. Offer clear paths for career advancement within your organization. Encourage open communication and actively seek feedback from your staff on how to improve processes and working conditions. When employees feel valued and see a future for themselves in your restaurant, they're more likely to be engaged, productive, and committed to your business's success.

Effective scheduling is an often-overlooked aspect of maximizing employee productivity and profitability in the restaurant industry. Balancing labor costs with customer demand requires a nuanced approach that takes into account historical sales data, seasonal trends, and individual employee strengths. Utilize scheduling software that allows you to analyze past performance and predict future needs. This can help you avoid overstaffing during slow periods and ensure you have enough hands-on deck during peak times. Consider implementing a flexible scheduling system that allows employees to easily swap shifts or pick up extra hours when needed. This not only improves productivity by ensuring optimal staffing levels but also enhances employee satisfaction by providing greater work-life balance.

Regular performance reviews and feedback sessions are essential tools for maintaining and improving employee productivity. These should be structured, consistent, and focused on both recognizing achievements and identifying areas for improvement. Use the KPIs you've established as a basis for these discussions, but also consider qualitative factors such as teamwork, initiative, and customer feedback. Provide specific, actionable feedback that employees can use to enhance their performance. Set clear, achievable goals for each team member and track progress over time. This approach not only helps improve individual productivity but also aligns your staff's efforts with your restaurant's overall objectives, driving profitability across the board.

In conclusion, the relationship between employee productivity and business outcomes in the restaurant industry is both complex and critical. By implementing a comprehensive strategy that includes clear metrics, ongoing training, technological innovation, a positive work environment, effective scheduling, and regular performance feedback, you can create a high-performing team that directly contributes to your restaurant's profitability. Remember, your employees are your most valuable asset—investing in their productivity is investing in your business's future success.

At the end of the day, there are two KPI's that I believe to be the best. They are often spoken about independently from other areas of the business; however, opportunities are often missed when they are left on their own.

Covers Per Labor Hour (CPLH) and Sales Per Labor Hour (SPLH)

Effective management of CPLH/SPLH requires a combination of strategic planning, staff training, and technology. One approach to optimizing this metric is through predictive scheduling. By analyzing historical data and trends, managers can anticipate busy periods and adjust staffing levels accordingly. This ensures that the restaurant is neither understaffed nor overstaffed at any given time, helping to maintain an optimal CPLH/SPLH.

Another strategy involves cross-training staff to handle multiple roles. Servers can be trained to assist with hosting duties during peak times, and bartenders can help with serving tables if needed. This flexibility allows the restaurant to adapt to fluctuations in guest volume more efficiently, ensuring that service remains smooth and prompt.

Investing in technology can also enhance CPLH/SPLH. Modern point-of-sale (POS) systems can streamline order taking and payment processes, reducing the time servers spend on administrative tasks. Additionally, table management software can help hosts optimize seating arrangements, minimizing wait times and maximizing table turnover.

Regular training and performance reviews are essential for maintaining high standards of service while optimizing CPLH/SPLH. Staff should be trained not only in their specific roles but also in the overall guest experience. This includes understanding the importance of efficiency and how it impacts both customer satisfaction and the restaurant's bottom line.

Finally, it's crucial to maintain open lines of communication between management and staff. Employees should feel comfortable providing feedback on scheduling, workload, and any challenges they face. This collaborative approach can identify potential issues before they escalate, ensuring that the restaurant operates smoothly and efficiently.

By implementing these strategies, restaurants can achieve a balanced CPLH/SPLH that supports both operational efficiency and exceptional guest experiences.

The last recommendation that I will always make regarding productivity in restaurants is this. CPLH is the best metric to be used in the front of the house, while SPLH is the best metric to be used in the back of the house. It is also crucial to understand that these are incredibly powerful tools to use as strategies in order to accomplish the business' goals.

Recap and Actionable Steps

Boosting profitability in the restaurant industry requires a multifaceted approach that addresses various aspects of your business operations. Throughout this chapter, we've explored several key strategies that can significantly impact your bottom line. These methods, when implemented thoughtfully and consistently, have the potential to transform your restaurant's financial performance and create a more sustainable business model in an industry known for its razor-thin margins and high operational costs.

One of the most powerful tools at your disposal is menu engineering. This process involves analyzing the popularity and profitability of each menu item to make informed decisions about pricing, placement, and even which dishes to keep or remove. By strategically designing your menu, you can subtly guide customers towards higher-margin items while still providing value and satisfaction. This approach not only increases your average check size but also helps streamline your kitchen operations by focusing on dishes that are both popular and profitable.

Effective cost management is another critical component of boosting profitability. This goes beyond simply cutting corners or reducing portion sizes, which can negatively impact customer experience. Instead, it involves a thorough examination of your expenses, from food costs to utilities, and identifying areas where efficiency can be improved without compromising quality. This might include negotiating better deals with suppliers, implementing energy-saving measures, or reducing food waste through better inventory management and preparation techniques.

In today's digital age, leveraging technology is no longer optional for restaurants seeking to maximize profitability. Modern point-of-sale (POS) systems, inventory management software, and customer relationship management (CRM) tools can provide invaluable insights into your business operations, helping you make data-driven decisions. These technologies can streamline ordering processes, reduce errors, and even help predict busy periods, allowing you to optimize staffing levels and reduce labor costs without sacrificing service quality.

Perhaps one of the most overlooked aspects of profitability in the restaurant industry is the direct link between employee productivity and business outcomes. High turnover rates not only increase training costs but also negatively impact service quality and team morale. By investing in your staff through fair wages, comprehensive training programs, and clear paths for advancement, you can create a more stable, skilled, and motivated workforce. This investment often pays dividends in the form of improved customer service, increased efficiency, and ultimately, higher profitability.

Now, let's translate these insights into actionable steps you can take to boost profitability in your restaurant:

1. Conduct a thorough menu analysis: • List all menu items and calculate their food cost percentage. • Track the sales volume of each item over a specific period. • Identify your stars (high profitability, high popularity), puzzles (high profitability, low popularity), plowhorses (low profitability, high popularity), and dogs (low profitability, low popularity). • Redesign your menu to highlight stars and improve or remove dogs. • Experiment with pricing and description changes for puzzles to increase their popularity. • Consider ways to increase the profitability of plowhorses without affecting their popularity.

2. Implement a robust cost management system: • Review all supplier contracts and negotiate better terms where possible. • Implement a digital inventory management system to track stock levels and reduce waste. • Conduct regular energy audits and invest in energy-efficient equipment. • Train staff on portion control and proper food handling to minimize waste. • Consider cross-utilizing ingredients across multiple dishes to reduce inventory complexity and waste.

3. Embrace technology to enhance efficiency: • Invest in a modern POS system that integrates with inventory management and CRM tools. • Implement online ordering and reservation systems to streamline operations and capture valuable customer data. • Use data analytics to forecast busy periods and optimize staffing levels. • Consider tableside ordering technology to increase order accuracy and

table turnover rates. • Implement a loyalty program to encourage repeat business and gather customer insights.

4. Focus on employee productivity and retention: • Develop a comprehensive onboarding and training program for all new hires. • Implement a fair and transparent system for performance evaluations and pay increases. • Create clear career paths within your organization to encourage long-term commitment. • Regularly solicit and act on employee feedback to improve workplace satisfaction. • Offer performance-based incentives that align with your profitability goals.

5. Continuously monitor and adjust: • Set up a system to regularly review key performance indicators (KPIs) such as food cost percentage, labor cost percentage, CPLH, SPLH and average check size. • Conduct weekly profit and loss reviews to identify trends and areas for improvement. • Stay informed about industry trends and be willing to adapt your strategies accordingly. • Regularly seek customer feedback and be responsive to changing preferences and expectations. • Foster a culture of continuous improvement among your staff, encouraging them to identify and suggest ways to enhance efficiency and profitability.

By implementing these strategies and remaining committed to ongoing improvement, you can significantly boost your restaurant's profitability. Remember, the key to success in the competitive restaurant industry lies not just in serving great food, but in running a smart, efficient, and adaptable business. With patience, persistence, and a willingness to embrace change, you can create a thriving restaurant that stands the test of time and economic challenges.

Leadership Commitment to a People-First Approach

Problem Introduction

The restaurant industry has long been plagued by a leadership approach that often prioritizes short-term profits over long-term sustainability and employee well-being. This traditional mindset, deeply ingrained in many establishments, has led to a cycle of high turnover rates, diminished customer satisfaction, and ultimately, reduced profitability. It's a vicious cycle that has become all too familiar to those who have spent any significant amount of time working in restaurants, from the bustling kitchens to the front-of-house operations.

In countless establishments across the globe, leadership teams continue to adhere to outdated management practices that view employees as replaceable cogs in a machine rather than valuable assets worthy of investment and development. This approach manifests in various ways: minimal training programs, inflexible scheduling, lack of growth opportunities, and a general disregard for work-life balance. The consequences of such practices are far-reaching and detrimental to the entire ecosystem of a restaurant, affecting everyone from the dishwasher to the executive chef.

The impact of these common leadership approaches extends far beyond the immediate frustrations experienced by staff members. It creates a ripple effect that touches every aspect of the restaurant's operations and customer experience. When employees feel undervalued and unsupported, their motivation plummets, leading to decreased productivity and a noticeable decline in the quality of service provided to patrons. This, in turn, results in dissatisfied customers who are less likely to return or recommend the establishment to others, directly impacting the restaurant's bottom line and long-term viability in an increasingly competitive market.

The financial implications of high turnover rates cannot be overstated. The constant cycle of hiring and training new employees is a significant drain on resources, both in terms of time and money. According to industry studies, the cost of replacing a single employee can range from several thousand dollars to upwards of twice their annual salary, depending on their role and level of experience. This financial burden is particularly challenging for restaurants already operating on razor-thin profit margins, especially in the face of rising food costs and increasing competition from alternative dining options.

The need for a fundamental shift towards a people-first strategy in the restaurant industry has never been more apparent or urgent. This approach represents a complete paradigm shift in how leadership teams view and value their workforce. It's about recognizing that the success of a restaurant is inextricably linked to the well-being, satisfaction, and growth of its employees. A people-first strategy goes beyond simply offering competitive wages; it encompasses creating a work environment where employees feel respected, supported, and empowered to contribute their best efforts.

Implementing a people-first approach requires a multifaceted strategy that addresses various aspects of the employee experience. This includes developing comprehensive training programs that not only equip staff with the necessary skills to perform their jobs effectively but also provide clear pathways for career advancement within the organization. It involves creating flexible scheduling systems that respect employees' personal lives and commitments outside of work, recognizing that a healthy work-life balance is crucial for long-term job satisfaction and retention.

Most of the time, a people-first strategy emphasizes open communication channels between management and staff, fostering an environment where feedback is not only welcomed but actively sought out and acted upon. This approach helps to identify and address potential issues before they escalate, leading to a more harmonious and productive workplace. It also involves recognizing and rewarding exceptional performance, not just through monetary incentives but also through opportunities for growth and increased responsibilities.

By prioritizing the well-being and development of their workforce, restaurants can create a positive cycle that benefits all stakeholders. Satisfied employees are more likely to provide exceptional service, leading to increased customer satisfaction and loyalty. This, in turn, contributes to improved financial performance and stability for the restaurant, allowing for further investment in employee development and retention programs. It's a self-reinforcing cycle that stands in stark contrast to the negative spiral created by traditional, profit-first approaches.

The transition to a people-first strategy is not without its challenges. It requires a significant shift in mindset, particularly for leaders who have long adhered to more traditional management practices. It may also involve short-term investments in training, development programs, and improved working conditions. However, the long-term benefits far outweigh these initial costs, offering a path to sustainable success in an industry known for its volatility and high failure rates.

Defining a People-First Leadership Style

In the fast-paced world of restaurants, where the sizzle of pans and the clinking of glasses create a symphony of organized chaos, leadership often takes a back seat to the immediate demands of service. However, the most successful establishments have discovered a secret ingredient that elevates their business above the rest: a people-first leadership style. This approach, while not entirely new, represents a significant departure from the traditional, top-down management styles that have long dominated the industry.

At its core, people-first leadership is about recognizing that the heart of any restaurant isn't the food, the decor, or even the location—it's the people. This leadership philosophy places the well-being, growth, and satisfaction of employees at the forefront of all business decisions. It's a radical shift from viewing staff as interchangeable parts in a machine to seeing them as the vital, irreplaceable assets they truly are.

The characteristics of people-first leadership are multifaceted and deeply intertwined with the day-to-day operations of a restaurant. First and foremost, it involves active listening—not just hearing the words spoken by staff, but truly understanding their concerns, ideas, and aspirations. This means creating an environment where open communication is not just encouraged but is an integral part of the restaurant's culture, where feedback flows freely in both directions, and where every voice, from the dishwasher to the head chef, is valued and respected.

Empathy stands as another cornerstone of this leadership style. In an industry known for its high-stress environments and long hours, the ability to put oneself in the shoes of employees is invaluable. People-first leaders make a conscious effort to understand the challenges faced by their staff, both within and outside the workplace. They recognize that personal lives don't simply pause when an employee clocks in, and they strive to create flexible schedules and supportive policies that acknowledge the whole person, not just the worker.

Investment in employee development is a hallmark of people-first leadership that sets it apart from traditional practices. Instead of viewing training as a necessary evil or a one-time event, these leaders see it as an ongoing process of growth and empowerment. They actively seek out opportunities for their staff to learn new skills, take on additional responsibilities, and advance their careers within the restaurant or the broader industry. This might involve cross-training programs, mentorship opportunities, or even partnerships with culinary schools and hospitality programs to provide formal education and certification options.

Transparency in decision-making processes represents another key differentiator of people-first leadership. While traditional leadership models often operate on a "need-to-know" basis, keeping staff in the dark about the reasons behind policy changes or business decisions, people-first leaders strive for openness. They share the why behind the what, helping employees understand the broader context of their work and how it contributes to the restaurant's overall success. This transparency extends to financial matters as well, with some people-first leaders even implementing open-book management practices to give staff a clearer picture of the business's health and their role in its prosperity.

Recognition and appreciation form the bedrock of the people-first approach. Unlike traditional models that may rely on annual reviews or sporadic acknowledgments, people-first leaders make recognition a daily practice. They understand that a sincere "thank you" or a moment taken to highlight exceptional service can have a profound impact on morale and motivation. These leaders go beyond generic praise, offering specific, personalized recognition that demonstrates a genuine understanding and appreciation of each employee's unique contributions.

Perhaps one of the most striking differences between people-first leadership and traditional practices lies in the approach to problem-solving and decision-making. While traditional leaders might rely on their own expertise or a small circle of advisors, people-first leaders actively seek input from all levels of the organization. They create collaborative environments where problems are viewed as opportunities for collective growth and innovation. This collaborative approach not only leads to more creative solutions but also fosters a sense of ownership and investment among staff, as they see their ideas valued and implemented.

The commitment to work-life balance stands out as another defining characteristic of people-first leadership in the restaurant industry. Recognizing the physically and emotionally demanding nature of restaurant work, these leaders prioritize creating sustainable work environments. This might involve innovative scheduling practices, mental health support programs, or even reimagining the traditional structure of restaurant shifts to allow for more predictable hours and time off. By doing so, they not only improve the quality of life for their employees but also enhance the long-term sustainability of their workforce.

Ultimately, people-first leadership in the restaurant industry is about creating a culture of mutual respect, growth, and shared success. It's a departure from the authoritarian, high-pressure environments that have long been accepted as the norm. Instead, it offers a vision of restaurants as communities where every member is valued, supported, and given the opportunity to thrive. This approach not only benefits employees but also translates directly to improved customer experiences, as engaged and satisfied staff naturally provide better service.

As the industry continues to evolve and face new challenges, from labor shortages to changing consumer expectations, the principles of people-first leadership offer a roadmap for creating resilient, adaptable, and successful restaurant businesses. By prioritizing the human element in every aspect of operations, these leaders are not just running restaurants—they're building legacies that can weather any storm and emerge stronger on the other side.

Benefits of People-First Leadership

In the fast-paced world of restaurants, where the sizzle of pans and the clinking of glasses create a symphony of controlled chaos, a revolutionary approach to leadership is quietly transforming the industry. People-first leadership, a philosophy that places the well-being and growth of employees at the forefront of business strategy, is proving to be more than just a feel-good concept. It's a powerful catalyst for success that ripples through every aspect of restaurant operations, from the kitchen to the dining room, and ultimately to the bottom line.

At its core, people-first leadership in the restaurant industry is about recognizing that the true heart of hospitality lies not just in the food on the plate or the ambiance of the space, but in the people who bring it all to life. This approach involves a fundamental shift in how managers and owners view their staff – not as interchangeable parts in a well-oiled machine, but as valuable individuals with unique skills, aspirations, and potential. When leaders commit to nurturing their team's professional and personal growth, they unlock a wellspring of positive outcomes that can transform the entire dining experience.

One of the most immediate and tangible benefits of adopting a people-first leadership style is the remarkable boost in employee morale. In an industry notorious for its high-stress environment and demanding hours, staff members who feel genuinely valued and supported are more likely to approach their work with enthusiasm and dedication. This positive attitude is contagious, creating a workplace culture where teamwork flourishes and challenges are met with resilience and creativity. As a result, the entire restaurant ecosystem becomes more harmonious, with reduced conflicts, improved communication, and a shared sense of purpose among all staff members.

The ripple effect of heightened employee morale extends far beyond the kitchen doors and into the dining room, where it directly impacts customer satisfaction. Happy, engaged employees are naturally more attentive to guests' needs, more likely to go the extra mile in service, and better equipped to handle the inevitable hiccups that occur in any dining experience. This elevated level of service doesn't just meet customer expectations – it exceeds them, turning ordinary meals into memorable experiences that guests are eager to share and repeat. In an age where online reviews and social media can make or break a restaurant's reputation, the authentic warmth and attentiveness that stem from a people-first approach can be the difference between a one-time visit and a loyal customer base.

The long-term benefits of people-first leadership for a restaurant's brand reputation and loyalty are profound and far-reaching. In a competitive market where diners have countless options at their fingertips, restaurants that consistently deliver exceptional experiences backed by genuinely happy staff stand out from the crowd. Word-of-mouth recommendations, glowing online reviews, and repeat visits from satisfied customers all contribute to building a strong, positive brand image. This reputation not only attracts new customers but also helps to weather the inevitable storms that all businesses face, providing a cushion of goodwill during challenging times.

The loyalty fostered by a people-first approach extends beyond customers to employees themselves. In an industry plagued by high turnover rates, restaurants that prioritize their staff's well-being and growth often find themselves with a stable, committed workforce. This stability translates into significant cost savings on recruitment and training, allows for the development of deep institutional knowledge, and enables the cultivation of strong, lasting relationships with customers. Long-term employees who feel invested in their workplace become natural brand ambassadors, spreading positive word-of-mouth and attracting both customers and potential new hires through their genuine enthusiasm for their work.

The financial implications of a people-first leadership style, while sometimes less immediately apparent, are nonetheless substantial. Reduced turnover rates mean lower recruitment and training costs, while improved customer satisfaction leads to increased repeat business and higher average spend. The positive brand reputation built through exceptional service can reduce marketing costs over time, as satisfied customers become organic promoters of the restaurant. Additionally, engaged employees tend to be more productive and innovative, potentially leading to operational efficiencies and creative solutions that can further boost the bottom line.

Perhaps one of the most overlooked benefits of people-first leadership in the restaurant industry is its potential to attract and retain top talent. As word spreads about a restaurant's supportive work environment and commitment to employee growth, it becomes a magnet for skilled professionals looking for more than just a paycheck. This influx of talent can elevate the entire operation, from the quality of the food to the sophistication of the service, creating a virtuous cycle of excellence that further enhances the restaurant's reputation and success.

Implementing a people-first leadership approach is not without its challenges, particularly in an industry known for its tight margins and high-pressure environment. It requires a significant shift in mindset, consistent effort, and often, a willingness to prioritize long-term gains over short-term profits. However, the multifaceted benefits – from improved employee morale and customer satisfaction to enhanced brand loyalty and financial performance – make it a compelling strategy for restaurants looking to thrive in an increasingly competitive landscape. By recognizing that their greatest asset is their people, restaurant leaders can create not just successful businesses, but thriving communities that nourish both body and soul.

Implementing a People-First Strategy

Transitioning to a people-first approach in the restaurant industry requires a fundamental shift in mindset and operational practices. This transformation doesn't happen overnight; it's a gradual process that demands unwavering commitment from leadership and a willingness to challenge long-standing industry norms. The first step in this journey is to conduct a comprehensive assessment of your current organizational culture, identifying areas where employee needs are being overlooked or undervalued. This assessment should involve gathering feedback from staff at all levels, from dishwashers to managers, to gain a holistic understanding of the challenges and opportunities within your establishment.

Once you've gathered this crucial information, the next step is to develop a clear vision for what a people-first culture looks like in your specific context. This vision should encompass not only broad principles but also tangible, day-to-day practices that will bring these ideals to life. For instance, you might envision a workplace where every employee feels empowered to contribute ideas for improving customer service, or where work schedules are designed with consideration for personal lives and family commitments. It's essential to communicate this vision effectively to your entire team, ensuring that everyone understands the rationale behind the changes and feels invested in the transformation process.

Implementing a people-first strategy often requires significant changes to existing systems and processes. One critical area to address is your hiring and onboarding procedures. Instead of focusing solely on technical skills or experience, prioritize candidates who demonstrate strong interpersonal skills, empathy, and a genuine passion for hospitality. During the onboarding process, emphasize the importance of teamwork and mutual support, setting the tone for a collaborative work environment from day one. Additionally, consider implementing a mentorship program that pairs new hires with experienced staff members, fostering a sense of belonging and accelerating skill development.

Training and development play a crucial role in sustaining a people-first culture. Invest in comprehensive training programs that go beyond basic job skills to include topics such as emotional intelligence, conflict resolution, and effective communication. These soft skills are invaluable in creating a positive work environment and enhancing customer interactions. Demonstrate your commitment to employee growth by offering clear career progression paths and opportunities for cross-training in different roles. This not only improves job satisfaction but also builds a more versatile and resilient workforce capable of adapting to the ever-changing demands of the restaurant industry.

One of the most challenging aspects of implementing a people-first strategy is addressing deeply ingrained industry practices that prioritize short-term profits over employee well-being. For example, the common practice of scheduling split shifts or last-minute schedule changes can wreak havoc on employees' personal lives and contribute to burnout. To combat this, consider implementing more stable and predictable scheduling practices, even if it means sacrificing some operational flexibility. While this may seem counterintuitive at first, the long-term benefits of reduced turnover and increased employee satisfaction often outweigh the short-term challenges.

Another critical component of a people-first approach is creating a culture of open communication and feedback. Establish regular channels for employees to voice their concerns, ideas, and suggestions without fear of reprisal. This could take the form of anonymous suggestion boxes, regular team meetings, or one-on-one check-ins with managers. More importantly, demonstrate that this feedback is valued by taking visible action on employee suggestions whenever possible. When changes can't be implemented, provide clear explanations as to why, maintaining transparency and trust in the process.

Recognizing and rewarding employees for their contributions is essential in reinforcing a people-first culture. Move beyond traditional employee-of-the-month programs to create a more comprehensive recognition system that acknowledges various forms of excellence, from exceptional customer service to innovative problem-solving. Consider implementing peer-to-peer recognition programs that empower employees to celebrate each other's achievements, fostering a sense of camaraderie and mutual appreciation. Additionally, tie rewards to behaviors that align with your people-first values, reinforcing the importance of these principles in your organization.

As you implement these changes, be prepared for resistance from some quarters. Long-time employees or managers may be skeptical of new approaches, particularly if they've been successful under the old system. Address these concerns head-on by clearly communicating the benefits of the people-first approach, not just for employees but for the business as a whole. Share success stories from other restaurants or industries that have adopted similar strategies and be patient as your team adjusts to the new way of doing things. Remember that cultural change is a marathon, not a sprint, and maintaining consistency in your approach is key to long-term success.

Finally, it's crucial to regularly assess the impact of your people-first initiatives and be willing to make adjustments as needed. Develop key performance indicators that go beyond traditional metrics like sales and profit margins to include measures of employee satisfaction, turnover rates, and customer feedback. Regularly solicit input from your team on what's working well and what could be improved. By maintaining this iterative approach, you can continually refine your strategy to better meet the needs of your employees and, by extension, your customers.

Case Studies and Success Stories

The restaurant industry has long been plagued by high turnover rates and challenging profit margins, but a growing number of establishments are discovering the transformative power of people-first leadership. This approach, which prioritizes the well-being and development of employees, has yielded remarkable results for those brave enough to implement it. By examining the experiences of these trailblazers, we can glean valuable insights into the practical application and tangible benefits of putting people at the heart of restaurant operations.

One such success story comes from a mid-sized chain of casual dining restaurants that had been struggling with employee retention and customer satisfaction. The company's leadership team made a bold decision to overhaul their management philosophy, moving away from a top-down, numbers-driven approach to one that emphasized employee empowerment and personal growth. They instituted a comprehensive training program that went beyond basic job skills, focusing on leadership development, conflict resolution, and effective communication for all staff members, regardless of their position within the organization.

This investment in their people paid off handsomely. Within a year, employee turnover rates dropped by 40%, resulting in significant cost savings on recruitment and training. More importantly, the improved staff morale translated into enhanced customer experiences, leading to a 25% increase in positive reviews and a 15% boost in repeat business. The chain's success demonstrates that when restaurant leaders commit to nurturing their team's potential, the benefits ripple outward, touching every aspect of the business.

Another inspiring example comes from a high-end restaurant group known for its innovative cuisine and impeccable service. Faced with intense competition and rising operational costs, the ownership team realized that their greatest asset was their staff. They implemented a radical profit-sharing model, where a significant portion of the restaurants' earnings was distributed among all employees based on performance and tenure. This move not only incentivized excellence but also fostered a sense of ownership and pride among the staff.

The results were nothing short of remarkable. Employee engagement soared, with staff members actively seeking ways to improve efficiency and enhance the dining experience. The restaurants saw a 30% reduction in food waste as kitchen staff became more mindful of inventory management. Front-of-house teams began collaborating more effectively, resulting in smoother service and higher check averages. Within two years, the group's profitability had increased by 35%, despite the initial investment in the profit-sharing program.

These success stories underscore a crucial lesson: when restaurant leaders prioritize their people, they create a virtuous cycle of improvement that benefits everyone involved. By investing in employee development, fostering a sense of ownership, and creating opportunities for growth, these establishments have not only improved their bottom line but have also cultivated a more sustainable and fulfilling work environment. The ripple effects of this approach extend far beyond the walls of the restaurant, influencing the broader community and potentially reshaping the industry's reputation.

It's important to note that the transition to a people-first approach is not without its challenges. Many of these success stories involved initial resistance from middle management or skepticism from long-time employees accustomed to more traditional hierarchies. Overcoming these obstacles required unwavering commitment from leadership, clear communication of the vision, and patience as the new culture took root.

In some cases, it meant parting ways with team members who were unable or unwilling to adapt to the new philosophy.

One particularly instructive case comes from a family-owned restaurant that had been operating for three generations. The current owner, recognizing the need for change, implemented a mentorship program that paired experienced staff with newer employees. This not only facilitated knowledge transfer but also helped bridge generational gaps within the team. The program fostered a sense of continuity and respect for the restaurant's history while encouraging innovation and fresh perspectives.

The lessons learned from these industry leaders are clear: a people-first approach is not just a feel-good philosophy, but a sound business strategy with measurable returns. By prioritizing employee satisfaction, development, and empowerment, restaurants can create a more stable, productive, and innovative workforce. This, in turn, leads to improved customer experiences, stronger brand loyalty, and ultimately, healthier profit margins. The success stories we've examined demonstrate that when restaurant leaders invest in their people, they're not just building a better workplace – they're laying the foundation for long-term success in an increasingly competitive industry.

Recap and Actionable Steps

The people-first approach in restaurant leadership represents a paradigm shift that places employees at the heart of business operations. This philosophy recognizes that a thriving workforce is the cornerstone of exceptional customer service and sustainable business growth. By prioritizing the well-being, development, and satisfaction of staff members, restaurants can create a positive ripple effect that extends to every aspect of their operations, from the quality of food preparation to the warmth of customer interactions.

At its core, people-first leadership is about fostering an environment where employees feel valued, heard, and empowered. It's a departure from the traditional top-down management style that has long dominated the restaurant industry, often characterized by rigid hierarchies and a focus on short-term profits at the expense of long-term employee retention and satisfaction. Instead, this approach emphasizes open communication, collaborative decision-making, and a genuine investment in the personal and professional growth of each team member.

The benefits of adopting a people-first strategy are manifold and far-reaching. When employees feel respected and supported, they're more likely to exhibit higher levels of engagement, productivity, and loyalty. This translates into lower turnover rates, which can significantly reduce the substantial costs associated with constantly hiring and training new staff – a perennial challenge in the restaurant industry. Remember that satisfied employees are more likely to provide exceptional service, leading to increased customer satisfaction and repeat business, which are crucial for a restaurant's long-term success and reputation in an increasingly competitive market.

Implementing a people-first approach requires a fundamental shift in mindset and practices. It involves creating a culture where every decision, from scheduling to menu development, is made with consideration for its impact on the staff. This might mean offering more flexible work hours to accommodate personal commitments, providing opportunities for skill development and career advancement, or simply ensuring that employees have a voice in decisions that affect their work environment. While the transition may present challenges, particularly in establishments accustomed to more traditional management styles, the long-term benefits far outweigh the initial hurdles.

Success stories from restaurants that have embraced this approach abound, showcasing improved employee retention, enhanced customer experiences, and stronger financial performance. These case studies serve as powerful testaments to the efficacy of people-first leadership, demonstrating that when restaurants invest in their people, they're ultimately investing in their own success. The lessons learned from these industry leaders underscore the importance of consistency, authenticity, and a willingness to adapt and evolve in response to employee feedback and changing industry dynamics.

To initiate a people-first strategy in your restaurant, consider the following actionable steps:

Conduct a comprehensive assessment of your current workplace culture, including anonymous surveys to gather honest feedback from employees at all levels.

Develop a clear vision for your people-first approach, outlining specific goals and the values that will guide your leadership decisions.

Implement regular, open forums for staff to share ideas, concerns, and suggestions, ensuring that every voice has the opportunity to be heard.

Create a robust employee development program that includes cross-training opportunities, mentorship initiatives, and clear pathways for career advancement within your organization.

Review and revise your packages to ensure they are competitive and reflect the value you place on your employees' contributions.

Establish a recognition program that celebrates both individual and team achievements, reinforcing the behaviors and attitudes that align with your people-first philosophy.

Invest in technology and tools that can streamline operations and reduce unnecessary stress on your staff, allowing them to focus on providing exceptional service.

Regularly assess the impact of your people-first initiatives through key performance indicators such as employee satisfaction scores, turnover rates, and customer feedback.

Lead by example, consistently demonstrating the values and behaviors you wish to see in your team, and be willing to roll up your sleeves and work alongside your staff when needed.

Foster a culture of continuous improvement by encouraging experimentation, learning from failures, and adapting your approach based on what works best for your unique team and restaurant environment.

By embracing these principles and taking concrete steps to prioritize your people, you can transform your restaurant into a workplace that not only attracts and retains top talent but also delivers exceptional experiences to your customers. Remember, the journey to becoming a truly people-first organization is ongoing and requires sustained commitment and effort. However, the rewards – a loyal, engaged workforce, satisfied customers, and a thriving business – are well worth the investment. As you embark on this transformative path, keep in mind that every positive change, no matter how small, contributes to building a stronger, more resilient restaurant that can weather the challenges of the industry and emerge as a leader in both employee satisfaction and customer service.

Continuous Education and Training for Staff

Problem Introduction

In the fast-paced world of restaurants, where flavors evolve and customer expectations shift like sand, continuous learning isn't just a buzzword—it's the secret sauce that keeps your establishment ahead of the curve. The restaurant industry, with its razor-thin margins and high-stakes service, demands a workforce that's not just trained but constantly evolving. Yet, despite this pressing need, many restaurants find themselves caught in a cycle of inadequate training programs that barely scratch the surface of what's truly needed to excel in this challenging environment.

The current landscape of employee training in the restaurant industry is often characterized by a patchwork approach that leaves critical gaps in knowledge and skills. Many establishments rely on outdated methods, such as brief orientations or shadowing experienced staff, which fail to provide the comprehensive understanding required to navigate the complexities of modern restaurant operations. This shortsighted approach to staff development not only hampers the potential for excellence in service and cuisine but also contributes to the

114

industry's notoriously high turnover rates, as employees feel underprepared and overwhelmed by the demands of their roles.

The consequences of these training gaps ripple through every aspect of restaurant operations, from the quality of food preparation to the nuances of customer interactions. Servers who lack in-depth knowledge about menu items or wine pairings miss opportunities to upsell and enhance the dining experience. Kitchen staff without proper training in food safety protocols or the latest culinary techniques may compromise both the quality and safety of the dishes they prepare. Managers who haven't been equipped with the skills to effectively lead and motivate their teams struggle to create the cohesive, high-performing environment necessary for success in this high-pressure industry.

The rapid technological advancements reshaping the restaurant landscape—from sophisticated POS systems to online ordering platforms—demand a workforce that's not just comfortable with technology but adept at leveraging it to improve efficiency and customer service. Yet, many training programs fail to address these technological competencies, leaving staff ill-equipped to handle the digital tools that are becoming increasingly central to restaurant operations. This technological gap not only hinders operational efficiency but also puts restaurants at a competitive disadvantage in an industry where digital savvy can make or break the customer experience.

The importance of continuous learning in the restaurant industry extends beyond just keeping up with trends or mastering new technologies. It's about creating a culture of excellence and innovation that permeates every aspect of the business. When staff members are engaged in ongoing education and skill development, they're more likely to feel invested in their roles and committed to the success of the restaurant. This sense of investment translates into lower turnover rates, higher job satisfaction, and ultimately, a better dining experience for customers. In an industry where the difference between success and failure can often be measured in the smallest details of service and quality, a well-trained, continuously learning staff is not just an asset— it's a necessity.

Addressing these gaps in employee training and development requires a fundamental shift in how restaurants approach staff education. It's not enough to simply offer more training; the nature and quality of that training must evolve to meet the complex demands of the modern restaurant industry. This means developing comprehensive, ongoing learning programs that cover not just the basics of food service and preparation, but also go into areas like customer psychology, conflict resolution, and the finer points of culinary arts and beverage knowledge. It means embracing new technologies and methodologies in training delivery, from interactive e-learning platforms to hands-on workshops led by industry experts.

The challenge—and opportunity—lies in creating a learning ecosystem within your restaurant that not only addresses the current gaps in training but anticipates future needs. This proactive approach to staff development can transform your restaurant from a workplace into a learning organization, where every interaction and experience becomes an opportunity for growth and improvement. By investing in the continuous education of your staff, you're not just improving their skills—you're building a foundation for long-term success in an industry where adaptation and excellence are the keys to survival and prosperity.

Developing a Comprehensive Training Program

A well-structured training program forms the backbone of a successful restaurant operation, serving as the catalyst for employee growth and organizational excellence. The components of an effective training program are multifaceted, encompassing both technical skills and soft skills that are crucial for thriving in the fast-paced, customer-centric environment of the restaurant industry. At its core, a comprehensive training program should address the fundamental aspects of food safety, hygiene protocols, and proper handling of kitchen equipment, ensuring that every staff member, regardless of their role, has a solid foundation in these critical areas that directly impact the health and safety of both customers and colleagues.

Beyond these basics, an effective training program goes into the nuances of customer service, teaching staff how to anticipate guest needs, handle complaints with grace, and create memorable dining experiences that keep patrons coming back. This involves role-playing exercises, scenario-based training, and real-time feedback mechanisms that allow employees to practice and refine their interpersonal skills in a supportive environment. Additionally, the program should cover the intricacies of menu knowledge, including ingredients, preparation methods, and potential allergens, empowering staff to confidently answer customer queries and make informed recommendations.

For kitchen staff, the training program expands to include advanced culinary techniques, plating aesthetics, and the efficient use of specialized equipment. This might involve hands-on workshops led by experienced chefs, video tutorials demonstrating complex cooking processes, and regular taste tests to ensure consistency in flavor profiles across different shifts and locations. Front-of-house staff, on the other hand, benefit from training modules focused on upselling techniques, wine pairing fundamentals, and the art of creating a welcoming ambiance that aligns with the restaurant's brand identity.

Tailoring training to meet the needs of different roles is paramount in maximizing the effectiveness of the program and ensuring that each employee receives the most relevant and applicable knowledge for their position. This customized approach begins with a thorough analysis of each role's responsibilities, challenges, and growth opportunities within the restaurant ecosystem. For instance, bartenders require specialized training in mixology, alcohol safety laws, and efficient bar management, while hosts need to master reservation systems, seating strategies, and techniques for managing wait times during peak hours.

Management-level staff should receive additional training in leadership skills, conflict resolution, and financial management to effectively oversee operations and mentor their teams. This might include workshops on creating staff schedules, managing inventory, analyzing profit and loss statements, and implementing strategies to boost overall restaurant performance. By providing role-specific training, restaurants can ensure that each employee is equipped with the precise skills and knowledge needed to excel in their position, leading to improved job satisfaction and reduced turnover rates.

To maximize the impact of role-tailored training, consider implementing a mentorship program where experienced staff members are paired with newer employees in similar positions. This approach not only facilitates knowledge transfer but also fosters a sense of camaraderie and shared responsibility among team members. Cross-training initiatives can be introduced to give employees a broader understanding of the restaurant's operations, enabling them to step into different roles when needed and promoting a more versatile and resilient workforce.

The development of a comprehensive training program should be an ongoing, iterative process that evolves with the changing needs of the restaurant industry and the specific challenges faced by your establishment. Regular assessments of training effectiveness, coupled with feedback from both staff and customers, can help identify areas for improvement and ensure that the program remains relevant and impactful. Consider establishing a dedicated training team or appointing a training coordinator responsible for overseeing the continuous refinement and delivery of the program.

Incorporating a mix of learning methodologies is crucial in catering to diverse learning styles and maximizing knowledge retention. This could include a combination of traditional classroom-style instruction, hands-on practical sessions, e-learning modules that can be accessed at the employee's convenience, and gamified learning experiences that make the training process more engaging and interactive. By offering a variety of learning formats, you can ensure that the training program remains accessible and effective for all staff members, regardless of their preferred learning style or schedule constraints.

As you develop and refine your training program, remember that its success hinges on consistent implementation and unwavering commitment from all levels of management. Make training a non-negotiable aspect of your restaurant's culture, allocating dedicated time and resources to ensure that every employee has the opportunity to participate fully in the program. By prioritizing comprehensive and tailored training, you're not just investing in your staff's skills; you're cultivating a team of knowledgeable, confident professionals who will drive your restaurant's success and set new standards of excellence in the industry.

Leveraging Technology in Training

The restaurant industry has long been known for its traditional, hands-on approach to training. However, as technology continues to reshape every aspect of our lives, it's time for restaurants to embrace digital tools and platforms to enhance their training programs. By leveraging technology, restaurants can not only streamline their training processes but also provide more engaging, accessible, and effective learning experiences for their staff.

One of the most significant advantages of using digital tools for training delivery is the ability to offer on-demand learning. This means that employees can access training materials at any time, from anywhere, using their smartphones, tablets, or computers. This flexibility is particularly valuable in the fast-paced restaurant environment, where scheduling conflicts often make it challenging to gather all staff members for in-person training sessions.

Learning management systems (LMS) are powerful platforms that can revolutionize your restaurant's training program. These systems allow you to create, organize, and deliver training content in various formats, including videos, interactive modules, quizzes, and assessments. With an LMS, you can easily track employee progress, identify areas where individuals may need additional support, and ensure that all staff members complete required training modules. This level of oversight and accountability is crucial for maintaining consistent service standards and compliance with food safety regulations across your entire operation.

Video-based training has become increasingly popular in the restaurant industry, and for good reason. Visual demonstrations of proper techniques, from food preparation to customer service interactions, can be far more effective than written instructions alone. Consider creating a library of short, focused video tutorials covering various aspects of your restaurant's operations. These videos can serve as valuable reference materials that staff can revisit whenever they need a refresher on specific procedures or techniques.

Virtual reality (VR) and augmented reality (AR) technologies are pushing the boundaries of what's possible in restaurant training. While these technologies may seem futuristic or out of reach for some establishments, they're becoming more accessible and affordable. VR simulations can provide immersive training experiences that allow staff to practice complex tasks or handle challenging customer scenarios in a risk-free environment. AR applications, on the other hand, can overlay digital information onto the real world, providing real-time guidance and information to employees as they work.

Gamification is another powerful tool that can make training more engaging and enjoyable for your staff. By incorporating game-like elements such as points, badges, leaderboards, and rewards into your training program, you can tap into employees' natural competitiveness and desire for achievement. This approach not only makes learning more fun but also encourages staff to actively participate in their own development and strive for excellence in their roles.

Mobile apps designed specifically for restaurant training can be incredibly useful for delivering bite-sized learning experiences. These apps can include features like daily quizzes, product knowledge flashcards, or short lessons on service techniques. By breaking down training content into small, easily digestible chunks, you make it more likely that employees will engage with the material regularly, reinforcing their learning over time.

Online collaboration tools and social learning platforms can foster a sense of community and peer-to-peer learning among your staff. These platforms allow employees to share their experiences, ask questions, and offer advice to one another. This type of collaborative learning can be particularly valuable in the restaurant industry, where experienced staff members often have a wealth of practical knowledge to share with their colleagues.

When implementing technology-based training solutions, it's important to remember that not all employees may be equally comfortable with digital tools. Provide adequate support and guidance to ensure that all staff members can access and use the training resources effectively. This might include offering in-person tutorials on how to use the new systems or designating tech-savvy team members as "digital mentors" to assist their colleagues.

While leveraging technology in training offers numerous benefits, it's crucial to strike a balance between digital and hands-on learning experiences. The restaurant industry is inherently tactile and interpersonal, so make sure to complement your digital training efforts with practical, real-world application. Use technology to enhance and support traditional training methods rather than completely replacing them.

As you integrate technology into your training program, continuously gather feedback from your staff on the effectiveness of different tools and approaches. Use this input to refine and improve your training strategies over time, ensuring that you're providing the most relevant and impactful learning experiences possible. By embracing technology in your training efforts, you'll be better equipped to develop a skilled, knowledgeable, and confident workforce that can deliver exceptional service and drive your restaurant's success in an increasingly competitive industry.

Measuring the Impact of Training

In the fast-paced world of restaurants, where every second counts and every customer interaction matters, the importance of effective staff training cannot be overstated. However, simply implementing a training program isn't enough. To truly understand its value and continuously improve its effectiveness, restaurant owners and managers must measure the impact of their training initiatives. This process involves carefully selecting and tracking specific metrics that align with the restaurant's goals and objectives, as well as establishing feedback mechanisms to gather insights from both staff and customers.

One of the most crucial metrics to consider when evaluating the effectiveness of a training program is the improvement in employee performance. This can be measured through a variety of indicators, such as increased sales per employee, reduced customer complaints, increased CPLH or improved efficiency in food preparation and service times. For example, a restaurant might track the average time it takes for a server to greet a table after being seated, or the number of menu items a server can accurately describe without referring to notes. These metrics provide tangible evidence of how well employees are applying the knowledge and skills they've gained through training.

Another important aspect to consider is the impact of training on employee retention rates. The restaurant industry is notorious for its high turnover, which can be incredibly costly for businesses. By tracking retention rates before and after implementing a comprehensive training program, restaurant owners can gauge whether their investment in employee development is paying off in terms of increased loyalty and job satisfaction. This data can be further broken down by department or role to identify areas where training might be particularly effective or where additional focus may be needed.

Customer satisfaction is arguably the most critical metric for any restaurant, and it's intrinsically linked to the quality of staff training. Implementing a system to regularly collect and analyze customer feedback can provide valuable insights into the effectiveness of your training program. This could involve traditional methods such as comment cards or more modern approaches like post-dining email surveys or social media monitoring. Pay close attention to trends in customer ratings and comments related to staff knowledge, friendliness, and overall service quality. A noticeable improvement in these areas following the implementation of a new training initiative is a strong indicator of its success.

Financial metrics also play a crucial role in measuring the impact of training. While it may be tempting to focus solely on the cost of training programs, it's essential to consider the return on investment (ROI) as well. This involves comparing the expenses associated with training (including materials, instructor fees, and employee time) against the financial benefits, such as increased revenue, reduced waste, or improved operational efficiency. For instance, if a training program on upselling techniques results in a 10% increase in average check size, the financial impact can be substantial and easily quantifiable.

To gain a more comprehensive understanding of training effectiveness, it's important to establish feedback mechanisms that allow for continuous improvement of the training content and delivery methods. Regular check-ins with employees who have undergone training can provide valuable insights into which aspects of the program they found most helpful and which areas might need refinement. This could be done through one-on-one conversations, anonymous surveys, or group discussions during staff meetings. Encourage open and honest feedback by creating a safe environment where employees feel comfortable sharing their thoughts without fear of repercussions.

In addition to employee feedback, consider implementing a peer review system where more experienced staff members observe and provide feedback on the performance of recently trained employees. This not only helps identify areas where the training may have fallen short but also reinforces the importance of continuous learning and improvement throughout the organization. It can also be an effective way to identify potential trainers or mentors within your existing staff, further enhancing the overall learning culture in your restaurant.

As you collect and analyze these various metrics and feedback, it's crucial to establish a regular review process to assess the overall effectiveness of your training program. This might involve quarterly meetings with key stakeholders to discuss trends, identify areas for improvement, and make data-driven decisions about future training initiatives. By taking a systematic approach to measuring the impact of training, restaurant owners and managers can ensure that their investment in employee development is yielding tangible results and contributing to the overall success of their business.

Remember that measuring the impact of training is not a one-time event but an ongoing process. As your restaurant evolves and faces new challenges, your training programs and the metrics you use to evaluate them should adapt accordingly. Stay open to new ideas and technologies that can help streamline the measurement process and provide more accurate insights. By consistently monitoring and refining your approach to training evaluation, you'll be better equipped to build a highly skilled, engaged workforce that can deliver exceptional dining experiences and drive your restaurant's success in an increasingly competitive industry.

Creating a Culture of Learning

In the fast-paced world of restaurants, fostering a culture of continuous learning isn't just a nice-to-have; it's a necessity for survival and success. This environment, where knowledge is valued and personal growth is encouraged, can transform your establishment from a mere workplace into a thriving hub of innovation and excellence. The benefits of such a culture extend far beyond the immediate improvement in skills – it enhances employee satisfaction, reduces turnover, and ultimately leads to a better dining experience for your customers.

To create this culture, start by leading by example. As a manager or owner, your attitude towards learning sets the tone for the entire organization. Demonstrate your commitment to personal growth by actively participating in industry conferences, workshops, or online courses. Share your experiences and newfound knowledge with your team, encouraging them to do the same. This openness to learning at all levels breaks down hierarchical barriers and creates an environment where everyone feels empowered to contribute ideas and seek out new information.

Implement a mentorship program within your restaurant. Pair seasoned staff members with newer employees, fostering relationships that go beyond the typical training period. These mentorships can be structured around specific skills or general career development. For instance, a veteran chef could mentor a promising line cook, sharing not just cooking techniques but also insights into menu planning, ingredient sourcing, and kitchen management. This approach not only accelerates the learning process for newer staff but also reinforces the knowledge of experienced employees, creating a win-win situation that strengthens your team's overall expertise.

Create opportunities for cross-training within your restaurant. Encourage front-of-house staff to spend time in the kitchen, and vice versa. This not only builds empathy and understanding between different roles but also broadens each employee's skill set. A server who understands the intricacies of food preparation can better explain menu items to customers, while a line cook who's experienced the pressures of the dining room might be more responsive to special requests. This holistic understanding of restaurant operations cultivates a more flexible, adaptable workforce capable of handling various challenges.

Establish a regular schedule of in-house workshops and training sessions. These can cover a wide range of topics, from wine pairings and cocktail crafting to customer service techniques and conflict resolution. Invite local experts, such as sommeliers, mixologists, or even regular customers with relevant expertise, to lead these sessions. This not only provides valuable knowledge but also exposes your staff to different perspectives and networking opportunities. Make these sessions interactive and engaging – perhaps incorporate tastings, role-playing exercises, or hands-on demonstrations to keep everyone involved and excited about learning.

Leverage technology to support continuous learning. Create a digital library of resources accessible to all staff members. This could include training videos, industry articles, recipe collections, and even a forum for sharing tips and asking questions. Encourage staff to contribute to this knowledge base, recognizing those who actively participate. Consider implementing a learning management system (LMS) that allows employees to access training modules at their own pace, track their progress, and even earn certifications. This digital approach not only makes learning more accessible but also appeals to younger staff members who are accustomed to online education.

Recognize and reward ongoing professional development. Implement a system where employees can earn points or badges for completing training modules, attending workshops, or acquiring new certifications. These points could translate into tangible benefits such as bonus pay, extra time off, or first choice of shifts. Publicly acknowledge staff members who have shown exceptional growth or have gone above and beyond in their learning efforts. This could be done through a "Learner of the Month" program or by featuring their achievements in staff meetings or on your restaurant's social media channels.

Encourage your staff to set personal learning goals and provide the support needed to achieve them. During regular performance reviews, discuss not just their current performance but also their aspirations and areas where they want to grow. Work together to create a personalized development plan that aligns with both their interests and the needs of your restaurant. This might involve enrolling them in external courses, assigning them special projects, or giving them opportunities to shadow more experienced staff in roles they're interested in pursuing.

Foster a culture of curiosity and experimentation. Create a "test kitchen" environment where staff can try out new recipes, techniques, or service ideas without fear of failure. Set aside time each week or month for these experiments and encourage all staff members to participate, regardless of their current role. This not only sparks creativity but also reinforces the idea that learning often involves trial and error. Celebrate both successes and failures as learning opportunities, discussing what worked, what didn't, and why.

Finally, make learning a part of your restaurant's identity. Include it in your mission statement and core values. Talk about your commitment to staff development in your marketing materials and job postings. This not only attracts employees who value personal growth but also sets you apart in the eyes of customers who appreciate dining at an establishment committed to excellence through continuous learning. By weaving education into the very fabric of your restaurant's culture, you create an environment where learning is not just encouraged but expected, setting the stage for ongoing innovation, improved service, and ultimately, greater success in the competitive world of hospitality.

Recap and Actionable Steps

Continuous education and training for staff in the restaurant industry isn't just a nice-to-have; it's a critical component of success in today's competitive landscape. Throughout this chapter, we've explored various strategies and approaches to enhance staff training, from developing comprehensive programs to leveraging technology and creating a culture of learning. Now, it's time to distill these insights into a practical framework that you can implement in your own establishment.

The importance of well-trained staff cannot be overstated. They are the face of your restaurant, the ones who interact directly with customers, and ultimately, they can make or break the dining experience. By investing in their development, you're not only improving their skills but also boosting their confidence, job satisfaction, and loyalty to your business. This, in turn, leads to better customer service, increased efficiency, and ultimately, a more profitable operation.

One of the key takeaways from our exploration is the need for a tailored approach to training. Every restaurant is unique, with its own culture, menu, and clientele. So, your training program should reflect these specificities. It's not about implementing a one-size-fits-all solution, but rather about crafting a program that addresses the particular needs of your staff and aligns with your restaurant's goals and values. This might mean focusing more on wine knowledge for fine dining establishments or emphasizing speed and efficiency for fast-casual concepts.

Technology has emerged as a powerful tool in the realm of staff training. From online learning platforms to virtual reality simulations, these digital solutions offer flexibility, consistency, and the ability to track progress in ways that traditional training methods simply can't match. However, it's crucial to remember that technology should complement, not replace, hands-on experience and personal interaction. The most effective training programs strike a balance between digital and traditional learning methods, leveraging the strengths of each to create a comprehensive learning experience.

Creating a culture of learning within your restaurant is perhaps the most challenging yet rewarding aspect of staff development. It requires a shift in mindset from viewing training as a one-time event to seeing it as an ongoing process of growth and improvement. This culture is fostered through consistent messaging, leading by example, and providing tangible incentives for professional development. When your staff sees learning as an integral part of their job rather than an obligation, they're more likely to take initiative in their own growth and contribute to the collective knowledge of the team.

Now, let's break down the process of building a robust training framework into actionable steps that you can implement in your restaurant:

• Conduct a thorough needs assessment: Begin by evaluating your current training practices and identifying gaps in knowledge or skills among your staff. This could involve surveys, performance reviews, and direct observation of daily operations. • Define clear learning objectives: Based on your needs assessment, establish specific, measurable goals for your training program. These should align with your restaurant's overall objectives and address the identified skill gaps. • Develop a comprehensive curriculum: Create a structured training plan that covers all essential aspects of your operation, from food safety and menu knowledge to customer service and conflict resolution. Ensure that the curriculum is modular, allowing for easy updates and customization. • Incorporate diverse learning methods: Blend traditional hands-on training with digital tools like e-learning modules, video demonstrations, and interactive quizzes. This variety caters to different learning styles and keeps the training engaging. • Implement a mentorship program:

Pair experienced staff members with newer employees to facilitate on-the-job learning and foster a sense of community within your team. • Leverage technology: Invest in a learning management system (LMS) to streamline the delivery and tracking of training content. This allows for self-paced learning and provides valuable data on employee progress. • Establish regular training sessions: Schedule ongoing training opportunities, such as weekly team meetings or monthly workshops, to reinforce key concepts and introduce new skills. • Create a feedback loop: Regularly solicit input from both trainers and trainees to continuously improve your training program. This could include post-training surveys, focus groups, or one-on-one discussions. • Recognize and reward learning: Implement a system that acknowledges and incentivizes staff who actively engage in training and demonstrate improved performance. This could range from verbal recognition to tangible rewards like bonuses or promotions. • Measure and analyze results: Use key performance indicators (KPIs) such as customer satisfaction scores, employee retention rates, and operational efficiency metrics to assess the impact of your training efforts. Use this data to refine your approach over time.

By following these steps and consistently prioritizing staff development, you'll be well on your way to creating a high-performing team that drives success in your restaurant. Remember, the investment you make in your staff's education and training will pay dividends in the form of improved service, increased efficiency, and a more positive work environment. It's a commitment that requires time, effort, and resources, but one that will ultimately set your restaurant apart in an industry where excellence is the expectation, not the exception.

Integrating Technology to Streamline Operations

Problem Introduction

The restaurant industry, a vibrant tapestry of flavors, cultures, and experiences, is facing a pivotal moment in its evolution. As we stand at the crossroads of tradition and innovation, the challenges of managing daily operations efficiently have become increasingly complex, demanding a fresh perspective and new solutions to age-old problems that have plagued establishments for decades, from the corner café to the Michelin-starred dining room.

In the fast-paced world of food service, where every second counts and every customer interaction can make or break your reputation, the struggle to maintain smooth operations is real and relentless. Picture a busy Friday night: servers darting between tables, the kitchen a cacophony of sizzling pans and shouted orders, while at the host stand, a growing line of hungry patrons checks their watches impatiently. In this controlled chaos, even the smallest inefficiency can snowball into major issues, affecting everything from food quality and customer satisfaction to staff morale and your bottom line.

The challenges are manifold and often interconnected, creating a complex web that can entangle even the most experienced restaurateurs.

Inventory management, for instance, is a delicate balancing act. Order too much, and you're left with spoilage and wasted resources; order too little, and you risk disappointing customers and losing sales. Then there's the scheduling nightmare - trying to ensure you have enough staff during peak hours without overstaffing during lulls, all while juggling time-off requests and last-minute callouts. Add to this the intricacies of table management, order accuracy, payment processing, and maintaining consistent quality across all dishes, and it's easy to see why many restaurant owners feel like they're constantly putting out fires rather than growing their business.

Enter technology - the game-changer that's revolutionizing how restaurants operate. In an industry that's been slow to embrace digital transformation, the role of technology in modernizing and streamlining processes can't be overstated. It's not just about replacing paper menus with tablets or accepting mobile payments; it's about fundamentally rethinking how we approach every aspect of restaurant management. From sophisticated POS systems that integrate ordering, inventory, and analytics, to AI-powered demand forecasting tools that help optimize purchasing and staffing, technology offers solutions to many of the pain points that have long plagued the industry.

But here's the challenge: implementing technology in a restaurant isn't as simple as downloading an app or plugging in a new gadget. It requires careful consideration, strategic planning, and often, a significant shift in mindset. The key is to view technology not as a cure-all, but as a powerful tool that, when wielded correctly, can enhance the human elements that make dining out special. It's about finding the sweet spot where efficiency meets hospitality, where data-driven decisions support rather than replace intuition and experience.

As we go deeper into the world of restaurant technology, we'll explore how to identify the areas of your operation that can benefit most from technological upgrades, how to choose the right solutions for your unique needs, and how to implement these changes in a way that empowers rather than alienates your staff. We'll look at real-world examples of restaurants that have successfully integrated technology to streamline their operations, boost their profits, and improve the dining experience for their guests. Most importantly, we'll discuss how to approach this digital transformation in a way that stays true to the heart and soul of your restaurant - because at the end of the day, technology should enhance, not replace, the human touch that makes dining out such a special experience.

Identifying Areas for Technological Integration

In the fast-paced world of restaurants, efficiency is the name of the game. Every second counts, every movement matters, and every decision can make or break your bottom line. As we dive into the realm of technological integration, it's crucial to understand that this isn't about replacing the human touch that makes dining experiences special.

Rather, it's about enhancing our capabilities, streamlining our processes, and ultimately creating more time and space for genuine human connections with our guests and staff.

The first step in this journey is to take a hard look at your current operations. This isn't a quick glance or a cursory review; it's a deep dive into every nook and cranny of your restaurant's daily functions. Start by shadowing your staff for a full day, from the moment the first employee arrives to prep the kitchen to the final lock-up at night. Pay close attention to the tasks that seem to eat up the most time or cause the most frustration. These are your prime candidates for technological upgrades.

One area that often benefits immensely from technological integration is the ordering system. If your servers are still jotting down orders on notepads and running back and forth to the kitchen, you're missing out on a significant opportunity for improvement. Modern point-of-sale (POS) systems can revolutionize this process, allowing servers to input orders directly into handheld devices that instantly communicate with the kitchen. This not only speeds up service but also reduces errors and improves communication between front and back of house.

Inventory management is another critical area where technology can make a world of difference. The days of manually counting stock and guessing your order quantities should be long behind us. Advanced inventory systems can track usage in real-time, predict future needs based on historical data, and even automate reordering processes. This level of precision not only saves time but can significantly reduce waste and overordering, directly impacting your bottom line. As I mentioned before, I use and recommend Margin Edge as the platform of choice for this.

Reservation systems are yet another aspect of restaurant operations that can benefit tremendously from technological upgrades. If you're still managing reservations with a pen and paper or even a basic spreadsheet, you're likely missing out on valuable opportunities. Modern reservation platforms can not only streamline the booking process but also gather crucial customer data, manage table turnover more efficiently, and even help with targeted marketing efforts. Open Table is the leader in this area, and the platform offers features that can make everything from planning the seating chart, to driving repeat visits easier. We use Open Table non-stop every day and the ROI on the platform is outstanding.

Employee scheduling and time tracking are often overlooked areas when it comes to technological integration, but they can have a massive impact on both operational efficiency and staff satisfaction. Automated scheduling systems can take into account employee availability, skill sets, and labor laws to create optimal schedules. They can also make it easy for staff to swap shifts or request time off, reducing the administrative burden on managers and improving overall workforce management.

Customer relationship management (CRM) systems are becoming increasingly important in the restaurant industry. These tools can help you track customer preferences, dining history, and even allergies or dietary restrictions. By leveraging this data, you can provide more personalized service, tailor your marketing efforts, and build stronger, long-lasting relationships with your guests. In an industry where repeat business is crucial, the insights provided by a good CRM system can be invaluable.

Kitchen display systems (KDS) are another technological upgrade that can significantly improve operations. These systems replace traditional paper tickets with digital displays, allowing for better organization of orders, clearer communication between front and back of house, and real-time tracking of order status. This can lead to faster service times, reduced errors, and a smoother overall kitchen operation.

Online ordering and delivery integration is no longer a luxury but a necessity in today's restaurant landscape. If you haven't already, consider implementing a robust online ordering system that integrates seamlessly with your POS and kitchen operations. This can open up new revenue streams and help you reach customers who prefer to dine at home.

Finally, don't overlook the potential of data analytics tools. These systems can help you make sense of the vast amount of data your restaurant generates daily. From sales trends and menu performance to customer behavior and staff productivity, the insights provided by these tools can inform strategic decisions and help you stay ahead of the competition. My recommendation here is always Hatch Insights, as they are the best I have seen for insights in one minute or less without having to click through a bunch of reports to find an answer.

As you assess these areas for potential technological integration, remember that the goal is not to implement technology for its own sake. Each upgrade should serve a specific purpose and address a real need in your operations. It's also crucial to consider how different systems will work together. The most effective technological solutions are those that integrate seamlessly with each other, creating a cohesive ecosystem rather than a patchwork of disconnected tools.

Choosing the Right Technology Solutions

In the ever-evolving landscape of the restaurant industry, selecting the appropriate technology solutions can make or break your business. The right tools can streamline operations, boost efficiency, and ultimately lead to increased profitability. However, with the myriads of options available, it's crucial to approach this decision-making process with a clear strategy and a thorough understanding of your specific needs. If you are ever unsure of what systems to use, who to talk to, or how to navigate all of the options, send me an email at jim@benchmarksixty.com and I will do my best to answer your questions.

When evaluating potential technology solutions for your restaurant, the first step is to conduct a comprehensive assessment of your current operations. This involves identifying pain points, bottlenecks, and areas where manual processes are slowing down your team or leading to errors. By pinpointing these issues, you can prioritize which aspects of your business would benefit most from technological intervention. For instance, if your kitchen staff is consistently struggling to keep up with orders during peak hours, a kitchen display system might be a game-changer. On the other hand, if your front-of-house team is spending too much time manually inputting reservations, an automated reservation system could free up valuable hours and reduce booking errors.

Once you've identified your primary needs, it's time to establish clear criteria for selecting the right technology tools. Compatibility with your existing systems should be at the top of this list. A new piece of software might seem perfect on paper, but if it doesn't integrate seamlessly with your current point-of-sale system or inventory management tools, it could create more problems than it solves. Scalability is another critical factor to consider. As your restaurant grows and evolves, your technology should be able to grow with you. Look for solutions that offer tiered pricing plans or modular features that can be added as your needs change.

Cost is, of course, a significant consideration, but it's essential to look beyond the initial price tag. Consider the total cost of ownership, which includes factors like ongoing subscription fees, maintenance costs, and potential hardware upgrades. Sometimes, a more expensive solution upfront can lead to significant savings in the long run through increased efficiency and reduced labor costs. Additionally, don't underestimate the importance of user-friendliness. Even the most powerful software is useless if your staff finds it too complicated to use effectively. Look for intuitive interfaces and robust training resources to ensure smooth adoption across your team.

Now, let's go into some of the popular software and systems that are making waves in the restaurant industry. Point-of-sale (POS) systems have come a long way from simple cash registers. Modern POS solutions typically offer features like tableside ordering, real-time inventory tracking, and detailed sales analytics. These comprehensive platforms can serve as the backbone of your restaurant's technology ecosystem, integrating with other tools to provide a seamless operational flow.

For inventory management, solutions like Margin Edge can help you keep track of stock levels, automate ordering processes, and even predict future inventory needs based on historical data. These tools can significantly reduce food waste and prevent costly overordering or stockouts. When it comes to reservations and customer management, platforms like OpenTable not only streamline the booking process but also provide valuable customer data and marketing opportunities.

Kitchen management systems are another area where technology is making a significant impact. Tools like a KDS (Kitchen Display System) can replace traditional paper tickets, improving communication between front-of-house and back-of-house staff. These systems can prioritize orders, estimate preparation times, and even integrate with delivery platforms to manage off-premise orders efficiently.

Employee scheduling and management software can simplify the often-complex task of creating staff schedules, tracking time and attendance, and managing labor costs. These tools often include features for team communication and performance tracking, helping to improve overall staff management and potentially reduce turnover. I definitely have a few favorites here, so don't hesitate to reach out if you are wondering which one to use.

As you evaluate these options, it's crucial to reach out to vendors for demonstrations and, if possible, trial periods. Many software providers offer free trials or limited-time access to their full suite of features. Take advantage of these opportunities to test the solutions in your real-world environment. Involve key staff members in the trial process to get their feedback and ensure the technology will be embraced by those who will use it daily.

Remember, the goal of integrating technology into your restaurant operations is not just to have the latest gadgets, but to solve real problems and create tangible improvements in efficiency, customer satisfaction, and profitability. By carefully assessing your needs, setting clear criteria, and thoroughly evaluating your options, you can choose technology solutions that will truly transform your restaurant's operations and set you up for long-term success in an increasingly competitive industry.

Training Staff to Use New Technologies

Introducing new technologies in a restaurant environment can be a game-changer, but it's not without its challenges. The success of any technological integration hinges on how well your staff can adapt to and utilize these new tools. Effective training is the cornerstone of this adaptation process, ensuring that your team not only understands how to use the new systems but also appreciates the benefits they bring to their daily work.

When implementing new technologies, it's crucial to start with a comprehensive training plan. This plan should outline the specific technologies being introduced, the timeline for implementation, and the expected outcomes. Begin by identifying key staff members who can serve as "technology champions" within your organization. These individuals should be naturally tech-savvy and enthusiastic about the changes, as they'll play a vital role in supporting their colleagues throughout the transition.

One effective approach to training is to break down the process into manageable modules. Start with the basics and gradually build up to more complex functionalities. For instance, if you're introducing a new point-of-sale system, begin with simple tasks like entering orders and processing payments before moving on to more advanced features like inventory management or customer loyalty programs. This step-by-step approach allows staff to build confidence and competence over time, reducing the likelihood of overwhelm and resistance.

Hands-on practice is invaluable when it comes to learning new technologies. Set up dedicated training stations where staff can experiment with the new systems without the pressure of live service. Encourage them to explore different scenarios they might encounter during a typical shift, such as modifying orders, handling split checks, or troubleshooting common issues. The more comfortable they become in a controlled environment, the smoother the transition will be when the technology goes live.

It's important to recognize that different staff members will have varying levels of technological proficiency and learning styles. Some may pick up new systems quickly, while others might require more time and support. Offer a variety of training formats to cater to these differences. This could include one-on-one sessions, group workshops, video tutorials, and written guides. By providing multiple avenues for learning, you increase the chances of successful adoption across your entire team.

Resistance to change is a natural human response, and it's something you're likely to encounter when introducing new technologies. Address this head-on by clearly communicating the benefits of the new systems. Explain how they will make jobs easier, improve customer service, or streamline operations. Be transparent about any challenges or temporary inconveniences that may arise during the transition period, but emphasize the long-term advantages. When staff understand the 'why' behind the changes, they're more likely to embrace them.

Create an open feedback loop during the training process. Encourage staff to voice their concerns, ask questions, and share suggestions. This not only helps identify areas where additional training might be needed but also gives employees a sense of ownership in the process. Consider implementing a mentorship program where more tech-savvy staff can support their colleagues, fostering a culture of collaborative learning and mutual support.

As you roll out the new technologies, be prepared for a temporary dip in efficiency. This is normal and should be factored into your implementation timeline. Consider running parallel systems for a short period, allowing staff to fall back on familiar methods while they gain confidence with the new tools. Gradually phase out the old systems as proficiency with the new technologies improves.

Ongoing support is crucial even after the initial training period. Schedule regular check-ins to address any lingering issues or questions. Keep training materials easily accessible for reference and consider creating a dedicated channel (such as a group chat or internal forum) where staff can share tips, ask questions, and troubleshoot problems together. This continuous learning approach ensures that the benefits of your technological investments are fully realized over time.

Remember that the goal of training is not just to teach the mechanics of using new technologies, but to instill a mindset of continuous improvement and adaptability. Encourage staff to explore and suggest new ways to leverage the technology to improve operations or enhance customer experience. This not only maximizes the value of your investment but also empowers your team to take ownership of their roles in driving the restaurant's success.

Monitoring and Evaluating Technology Impact

Integrating new technology into your restaurant operations is just the beginning of a transformative journey. The real challenge lies in understanding how these digital tools are affecting your business and whether they're delivering the expected results. This critical phase of monitoring and evaluation is often overlooked, yet it's the key to maximizing the return on your technology investments and continuously improving your operational efficiency.

To effectively track the impact of your newly implemented technologies, start by establishing clear, measurable objectives before the integration process begins. These goals should be specific to your restaurant's needs and aligned with your overall business strategy. For instance, if you've introduced a new point-of-sale system, you might aim to reduce order processing time by 30% or decrease billing errors by 50%. By setting these concrete targets, you create a benchmark against which you can measure the technology's performance.

Once your objectives are in place, it's time to dive into the data. Most modern restaurant technologies come equipped with robust analytics tools that provide a wealth of information about their usage and impact. Take the time to familiarize yourself with these reporting features and schedule regular reviews of the data they generate. This might involve analyzing metrics such as table turnover rates, average order values, or kitchen preparation times. The key is to focus on the indicators that directly relate to your predetermined goals and provide insights into the efficiency of your operations.

However, raw data alone doesn't tell the whole story. To gain a comprehensive understanding of how technology is impacting your restaurant, it's crucial to gather feedback from those who interact with it daily – your staff and customers. Conduct regular surveys or informal check-ins with your team to gauge their experiences with the new systems. Are they finding the technology intuitive and helpful, or are they encountering frustrations that hinder their work? Similarly, pay close attention to customer feedback, both direct and indirect. Have you noticed an uptick in positive reviews mentioning faster service or smoother ordering processes? These qualitative insights can provide valuable context to your quantitative data and help you identify areas where the technology might need fine-tuning.

As you collect and analyze this wealth of information, be prepared to make adjustments to your technology strategy. The restaurant industry is dynamic, and what works today might need tweaking tomorrow. If you find that certain features of your new system aren't being utilized as expected, consider additional training for your staff or reassessing whether that particular functionality aligns with your operational needs. Conversely, if a specific aspect of the technology is delivering exceptional results, explore ways to leverage it further or expand its use across other areas of your business.

Remember that the goal of monitoring and evaluation isn't just to justify your technology investments but to continuously optimize their performance. This might involve regular software updates, hardware upgrades, or even integrating complementary technologies to create a more comprehensive digital ecosystem for your restaurant. Stay informed about emerging trends and innovations in restaurant technology, and don't be afraid to experiment with new solutions that could further enhance your operations.

It's also important to recognize that the impact of technology on your restaurant extends beyond operational metrics. Consider how your digital tools are affecting less tangible aspects of your business, such as employee satisfaction and customer experience. Are your staff members spending less time on mundane tasks and more on meaningful guest interactions? Has the overall ambiance of your restaurant improved with the reduction of paper clutter and streamlined processes? These qualitative improvements can have a significant long-term impact on your restaurant's success and should be factored into your evaluation of technology effectiveness.

As you become more adept at monitoring and evaluating your restaurant's technology, you'll likely discover patterns and insights that can inform broader business decisions. For example, data from your inventory management system might reveal seasonal trends in ingredient usage, allowing you to optimize your purchasing and menu planning. Or analysis of your online ordering platform could uncover peak times for takeout orders, helping you adjust staffing levels accordingly. By viewing your technology not just as operational tools but as sources of valuable business intelligence, you can unlock new opportunities for growth and innovation in your restaurant.

Ultimately, the process of monitoring and evaluating technology impact in your restaurant is an ongoing journey of learning and improvement. It requires dedication, attention to detail, and a willingness to adapt. But by committing to this process, you'll ensure that your technology investments continue to deliver value, driving efficiency, enhancing customer satisfaction, and contributing to the long-term success of your restaurant in an increasingly digital world.

Recap and Actionable Steps

Technology integration in the restaurant industry isn't just about keeping up with the latest trends; it's about fundamentally transforming how we operate our businesses to meet the evolving demands of both customers and staff. Throughout this chapter, we've explored various aspects of integrating technology to streamline operations, from identifying areas ripe for technological upgrades to selecting the right solutions and training staff effectively. The impact of well-implemented technology on a restaurant's efficiency, profitability, and overall success cannot be overstated, especially in an industry where margins are notoriously thin, and competition is fierce.

One of the most critical takeaways from our discussion is the importance of a strategic approach to technology adoption. It's not about implementing every shiny new gadget or software that hits the market; rather, it's about carefully assessing your specific operational needs and challenges, then selecting technologies that directly address those issues. This might mean investing in a robust point-of-sale system that integrates seamlessly with your inventory management and customer relationship management tools, or it could involve adopting a kitchen display system that revolutionizes how orders are communicated and fulfilled.

Another key point we've emphasized is the human element of technology integration. The most sophisticated systems in the world won't improve your operations if your staff aren't on board or adequately trained to use them. We've discussed strategies for overcoming resistance to change and effective training methods that ensure your team not only understands how to use new technologies but also appreciates the benefits these tools bring to their daily work. This human-centric approach to technology adoption is crucial for realizing the full potential of your investments and creating a more efficient, harmonious work environment.

As we wrap up this chapter, it's essential to remember that technology integration is an ongoing process, not a one-time event. The landscape of restaurant technology is constantly evolving, and staying competitive means being willing to adapt and innovate continually. This doesn't mean chasing every new trend, but rather staying informed about technological advancements that could significantly impact your operations and being open to experimenting with solutions that align with your business goals.

Now, let's distill the key insights from this chapter into actionable steps you can take to effectively implement technology solutions in your restaurant:

Conduct a comprehensive audit of your current operations, identifying pain points and inefficiencies that could be addressed through technology. This might involve analyzing customer feedback, staff surveys, and operational data to pinpoint areas where technology could make the most significant impact.

Research and evaluate technology solutions specific to the restaurant industry, focusing on those that address your identified needs. Consider factors such as scalability, integration capabilities with existing systems, user-friendliness, and vendor support when making your selections.

Develop a phased implementation plan for introducing new technologies. Start with one or two key areas to avoid overwhelming your staff and systems. This could mean beginning with a new POS system before moving on to kitchen management software or online ordering platforms.

Create a comprehensive training program for your staff, tailored to different roles and skill levels. Include hands-on practice sessions, written materials, and ongoing support to ensure everyone feels confident using the new systems.

Establish clear metrics for measuring the impact of your technology investments. This might include tracking improvements in order accuracy, table turnover rates, labor costs, or customer satisfaction scores. Regularly review these metrics to assess the effectiveness of your technology solutions and identify areas for further improvement.

Foster a culture of continuous learning and adaptation within your restaurant. Encourage staff to provide feedback on the new systems and be open to making adjustments based on their input and real-world performance data.

Stay informed about emerging technologies in the restaurant industry by attending trade shows, joining industry associations, and networking with other restaurateurs. This will help you anticipate future trends and stay ahead of the curve in terms of operational efficiency.

Regularly reassess your technology stack to ensure it continues to meet your evolving needs. Be prepared to upgrade or replace systems as your business grows or as more advanced solutions become available.

By following these steps and maintaining a strategic, thoughtful approach to technology integration, you can transform your restaurant operations, enhancing efficiency, improving the customer experience, and ultimately boosting your bottom line. Remember, the goal isn't to adopt technology for its own sake, but to leverage it as a powerful tool in creating a more successful, sustainable restaurant business that stands out in a crowded and competitive industry.

Building a Supportive and Inclusive Workplace Culture

Problem Introduction

In the fast-paced, high-pressure world of restaurants, the importance of a positive workplace culture cannot be overstated. It's the invisible force that can make or break your establishment, influencing everything from employee satisfaction and retention to customer experience and ultimately, your bottom line. Yet, despite its critical role, many restaurant owners and managers overlook this crucial aspect of their business, focusing solely on the tangible elements like menu quality, service speed, and profit margins.

The restaurant industry is notorious for its high turnover rates, with some estimates suggesting that employees change jobs as frequently as every few months. This constant churn not only disrupts operations but also bleeds your business dry through recurring recruitment and training costs. In fact, it creates a cycle of instability that can severely impact team morale, customer service quality, and overall operational efficiency. But here's the crux of the matter: much of this turnover can be directly attributed to a toxic or unsupportive workplace culture.

Common cultural issues plaguing the restaurant industry are as diverse as they are detrimental. From the hierarchical kitchen structure that can breed intimidation and fear, to the often-blurred lines between professional and personal relationships in close-knit teams, these problems can create a powder keg of tension just waiting to explode. Add to this the high-stress environment, long and often unsociable hours, and the physical demands of the job, and you have a recipe for employee burnout and dissatisfaction.

One of the most insidious cultural issues in restaurants is the normalization of toxic behavior. The "Old School" screaming chef, the manager who plays favorites, or the owner who treats staff as disposable – these stereotypes persist because they're rooted in real experiences. Such behaviors not only create a hostile work environment but also perpetuate a cycle of negativity that can spread through your entire organization like wildfire. Left unchecked, these issues can lead to decreased productivity, increased absenteeism, and a revolving door of staff that will drain your resources and reputation.

Another often-overlooked cultural problem is the lack of clear communication and feedback channels. In the hustle and bustle of a busy restaurant, it's easy for management to fall into a top-down, command-and-control style of leadership. However, this approach can leave employees feeling voiceless and undervalued, leading to disengagement and a disconnect between management's vision and the day-to-day reality on the restaurant floor. When staff don't feel heard or appreciated, they're far more likely to seek opportunities elsewhere, taking their skills, experience, and potentially even your regular customers with them.

The absence of growth opportunities and clear career paths within your restaurant can also significantly undermine employee satisfaction and productivity. Many enter the industry with passion and ambition, only to find themselves stuck in roles with little prospect for advancement or skill development. This stagnation can lead to a sense of futility and disillusionment, causing your best talent to look for greener pastures where they can grow and evolve professionally. By failing to nurture and develop your staff, you're not just losing valuable employees – you're potentially creating your future competition.

Inclusivity, or rather the lack thereof, is another critical cultural issue that can silently erode your workplace environment. In an industry as diverse as food service, it's crucial to create a space where everyone feels welcome and valued, regardless of their background, gender, race, or sexual orientation. However, many restaurants struggle with unconscious biases, clique formation, or even overt discrimination. These issues not only create a hostile work environment but can also lead to legal troubles and severe reputational damage in our increasingly socially conscious world.

Addressing these cultural issues isn't just about creating a nicer place to work – it's about building a sustainable, profitable business. A positive workplace culture can be your secret weapon in the competitive restaurant landscape. It can help you attract and retain top talent, boost productivity, enhance customer service, and ultimately drive your success. In the following sections, we'll dive deep into strategies for defining, implementing, and maintaining a supportive and inclusive culture that will transform your restaurant from just another workplace into a thriving community that people are proud to be part of.

Defining Your Culture

The culture of your restaurant is the invisible force that shapes every interaction, decision, and experience within your establishment. It's the heartbeat of your business, pumping life into every corner of your operation. But here's the challenge: many restaurant owners and managers struggle to articulate what their culture actually is, let alone how to shape it intentionally. This lack of clarity can lead to a disconnect between what you envision for your restaurant and the reality experienced by your staff and customers.

To define your culture effectively, start by taking a step back and observing your current environment. What are the unspoken rules that govern how people interact? How do your team members treat each other and your customers? What behaviors are rewarded, and which ones are discouraged? These observations will give you a baseline understanding of your existing culture, warts and all. It's crucial to be honest with yourself during this process, acknowledging both the positive aspects and the areas that need improvement.

Once you have a clear picture of your current culture, it's time to envision what you want it to be. This isn't about creating a utopian fantasy, but rather a realistic and aspirational vision that aligns with your business goals and values. Consider the type of experience you want to create for your customers and the work environment you want to foster for your employees. Do you want a fast-paced, high-energy atmosphere that prioritizes efficiency and quick service? Or are you aiming for a more relaxed, intimate setting where staff can take the time to build relationships with regular customers? Your cultural vision should be a natural extension of your overall business strategy, supporting and enhancing your operational goals.

With your vision in mind, the next step is to articulate your cultural values clearly and concisely. These values should be more than just buzzwords on a poster; they need to be actionable principles that guide decision-making at all levels of your organization. For example, if one of your values is "creativity," this might translate into encouraging staff to experiment with new menu items or innovative service techniques. If "teamwork" is a core value, you might implement cross-training programs or team-building activities to foster collaboration. The key is to make these values tangible and relevant to your day-to-day operations.

Once you've defined your cultural values, it's crucial to communicate them effectively to your entire team. This goes beyond simply posting them on the wall or including them in an employee handbook. You need to bring these values to life through stories, examples, and consistent reinforcement. Share anecdotes that illustrate each value in action, highlighting how they contribute to the success of your restaurant. For instance, if "customer-first" is one of your values, you might share a story about a server who went above and beyond to accommodate a guest with dietary restrictions, resulting in a glowing review and repeat business.

Alignment between your cultural values and your broader business goals is essential for long-term success. Your culture should support and enhance your operational objectives, not work against them. If your goal is to become known for exceptional fine dining experiences, a culture that prioritizes speed over quality would be counterproductive. Similarly, if you're aiming to create a family-friendly neighborhood spot, a culture that feels exclusive or intimidating would hinder your progress. Take the time to carefully consider how each aspect of your desired culture contributes to your overall business strategy.

As you work to define and articulate your culture, remember that this is an ongoing process, not a one-time event. Your culture will evolve as your business grows and changes, and it's important to regularly reassess and refine your cultural vision. Encourage feedback from your team and be open to making adjustments based on their insights and experiences. Your staff are on the front lines every day, and they often have valuable perspectives on what's working well and what could be improved.

Implementing cultural changes can be challenging, especially in an industry known for high turnover and intense pressure. Be patient and persistent in your efforts, recognizing that meaningful change takes time. Start by focusing on small, achievable wins that demonstrate the benefits of your cultural vision. For example, if you're working to create a more supportive environment, you might begin by implementing a peer recognition program or offering more flexible scheduling options. These tangible actions will help build momentum and buy-in from your team.

As you define and refine your restaurant's culture, keep in mind that authenticity is key. Your cultural values should reflect your genuine beliefs and aspirations, not just what you think sounds good on paper. Staff and customers alike can quickly spot insincerity, which can undermine all your efforts. Be true to your vision and values, and let them guide every aspect of your operation, from hiring decisions to menu design to customer service policies. When your culture is authentic and consistently reinforced, it becomes a powerful tool for attracting and retaining both staff and customers who share your values and vision.

Implementing Cultural Change

Cultural change in a restaurant is not an overnight process; it's a gradual evolution that requires careful planning, consistent effort, and unwavering commitment from every level of the organization. The first step in implementing cultural change is to clearly communicate the vision for the new culture to all employees, from the kitchen staff to the front-of-house team. This communication should be thorough, explaining not just what changes are being made, but why they're necessary and how they align with the restaurant's overall goals and values. It's crucial to articulate how these changes will benefit both the business and the employees themselves, as this understanding can significantly boost buy-in and reduce resistance to change.

Once the vision has been communicated, the next step is to lead by example. Restaurant owners and managers must embody the cultural changes they wish to see in their establishments. This means consistently demonstrating the behaviors and attitudes that reflect the desired culture, whether it's showing respect for all team members, promoting work-life balance, or fostering an environment of continuous learning and improvement. When leadership actively models the new culture, it sends a powerful message to the rest of the team about the seriousness and importance of these changes.

To further embed the new culture, consider implementing a mentorship program where experienced staff members who have embraced the cultural changes can guide and support newer employees. This not only helps to spread the new cultural norms more organically throughout the organization but also provides valuable professional development opportunities for your team. Additionally, regular team meetings and one-on-one check-ins can be used as platforms to reinforce cultural values, address any concerns or resistance, and celebrate successes as the new culture takes root.

Training programs play a crucial role in implementing cultural change. Develop comprehensive training modules that not only teach the technical skills required for various roles but also emphasize the soft skills and behaviors that align with the new culture. This might include workshops on effective communication, conflict resolution, or diversity and inclusion. Make these training sessions interactive and engaging, using role-playing exercises and real-life scenarios from your restaurant to make the learning more relevant and applicable. Consider bringing in external experts or using industry-specific training resources to add depth and credibility to your cultural change initiatives.

Another effective strategy for implementing cultural change is to align your hiring practices with your new cultural values. When recruiting new team members, look beyond just technical skills and experience. Seek out candidates whose personal values and work ethic align with your desired culture. During the interview process, ask behavioral questions that reveal a candidate's attitude towards teamwork, customer service, and adaptability. By bringing in new employees who are already a good cultural fit, you can accelerate the adoption of your new culture and create a more cohesive team.

Engaging employees in the change process is crucial for its success. Create opportunities for staff to provide input and feedback on the cultural changes. This could be through anonymous suggestion boxes, regular surveys, or open forum discussions. When employees feel their voices are heard and their ideas are valued, they're more likely to embrace and champion the new culture. This engagement can lead to valuable insights and ideas that management might not have considered, potentially improving the overall implementation of the cultural changes.

To reinforce the new culture, consider revising your reward and recognition systems to align with the desired behaviors and values. This might involve creating new categories for employee recognition that specifically highlight actions that embody the new culture. For example, you could introduce awards for exceptional teamwork, innovative problem-solving, or outstanding customer service. Make sure these recognitions are given regularly and publicly to reinforce their importance and inspire others to follow suit.

It's important to acknowledge that cultural change can be challenging and may face resistance from some team members. Be prepared to address this resistance with patience and understanding. Provide additional support and coaching to employees who are struggling with the changes. Sometimes, resistance stems from fear or misunderstanding, so open and honest communication can go a long way in alleviating concerns. However, if after sufficient time and support, certain individuals continue to actively resist or undermine the new culture, it may be necessary to have difficult conversations about their future with the organization.

Finally, remember that implementing cultural change is an ongoing process that requires continuous effort and refinement. Regularly assess the progress of your cultural change initiatives using both quantitative metrics (such as employee satisfaction surveys or turnover rates) and qualitative feedback from your team. Be prepared to make adjustments to your approach based on what's working well and what needs improvement. Celebrate milestones and successes along the way to maintain momentum and motivation. With persistence, patience, and a genuine commitment to creating a positive work environment, you can successfully implement lasting cultural change that transforms your restaurant into a thriving, supportive workplace where both employees and the business can flourish.

Maintaining an Inclusive Environment

In the fast-paced world of restaurants, where diverse teams come together to create unforgettable dining experiences, fostering an inclusive environment is not just a nice-to-have—it's a critical component of success. An inclusive workplace culture in the restaurant industry goes beyond mere diversity quotas; it's about creating an atmosphere where every team member, from the dishwasher to the head chef, feels valued, respected, and empowered to contribute their unique perspectives and talents. This kind of environment doesn't just happen by chance; it requires deliberate effort, thoughtful practices, and a commitment to continuous improvement.

To begin building a truly inclusive restaurant environment, start by examining your hiring practices. Are you casting a wide net to attract diverse candidates? Consider partnering with local community organizations, culinary schools with diverse student bodies, and job fairs in different neighborhoods. When reviewing applications, implement blind screening techniques to minimize unconscious bias. This could involve removing names and other identifying information from resumes before the initial review process. By doing so, you'll focus solely on qualifications and experience, giving every candidate a fair shot at moving forward in the hiring process.

Once you've assembled a diverse team, the real work of inclusion begins. Regular diversity and inclusion training for all staff members, from entry-level to management, is crucial. These sessions should go beyond surface-level discussions and go into topics like recognizing and addressing microaggressions, understanding different cultural perspectives on food and service, and creating an environment where everyone feels comfortable speaking up. Consider bringing in expert facilitators who can guide these conversations sensitively and productively, ensuring that all participants feel heard and respected throughout the process.

In the day-to-day operations of your restaurant, inclusivity should be woven into every aspect of the work environment. This means creating flexible scheduling options that accommodate different cultural and religious observances, offering menu items that cater to various dietary restrictions and cultural preferences, and ensuring that your restaurant's decor and ambiance reflect the diversity of your staff and customers. It's also crucial to establish clear channels for feedback and concerns, where employees can safely voice their thoughts without fear of retaliation. This could be in the form of anonymous suggestion boxes, regular one-on-one check-ins with managers, or even a dedicated diversity and inclusion committee comprised of staff members from various levels and departments within the restaurant.

Language plays a pivotal role in creating an inclusive environment. Encourage the use of gender-neutral terms in both customer-facing interactions and internal communications. For instance, instead of "guys" when addressing a table, train your staff to use inclusive alternatives like "folks" or "everyone." In the kitchen and back-of-house areas, promote the use of respectful language that doesn't alienate or marginalize any group. This extends to written materials as well—review your menus, training manuals, and employee handbooks to ensure they use inclusive language and avoid cultural stereotypes or assumptions.

Recognition and advancement opportunities should be equitable and transparent. Implement a clear, merit-based system for promotions and raises, and regularly review this system to ensure it's free from bias. Encourage mentorship programs that pair seasoned staff members with newer employees from diverse backgrounds, fostering a sense of belonging and providing pathways for career growth. Celebrate the diverse achievements and contributions of your team members, not just during designated months or holidays, but as an ongoing practice. This could involve featuring employee stories in your restaurant's marketing materials, social media, or even on your menu, highlighting the unique skills and experiences they bring to your establishment.

The benefits of cultivating a diverse and inclusive work culture in your restaurant are manifold and far-reaching. First and foremost, it leads to increased employee satisfaction and retention. In an industry plagued by high turnover rates, creating an environment where staff members feel valued and see a future for themselves can significantly reduce the costs associated with constant hiring and training. Also, a diverse team brings a wealth of perspectives, ideas, and problem-solving approaches to the table. This diversity of thought can lead to innovation in menu development, service techniques, and operational efficiencies, giving your restaurant a competitive edge in a crowded market.

An inclusive restaurant environment also resonates strongly with customers. In today's socially conscious world, diners are increasingly seeking out establishments that reflect their values. A visibly diverse staff and an atmosphere of inclusivity can attract a wider customer base, leading to increased patronage and positive word-of-mouth. When employees feel respected and valued, this positivity naturally extends to their interactions with customers, resulting in higher levels of service quality and customer satisfaction. This, in turn, can lead to better reviews, repeat business, and a stronger overall reputation for your restaurant.

Implementing these inclusive practices isn't without its challenges. It requires ongoing commitment, resources, and a willingness to confront and change long-standing industry norms. However, the long-term benefits—a more harmonious work environment, reduced turnover, increased creativity, and a loyal customer base—far outweigh the initial investment. By prioritizing inclusivity, you're not just creating a better workplace; you're positioning your restaurant for sustainable success in an increasingly diverse and socially aware market. Remember, true inclusivity is an ongoing journey, not a destination. Regularly assess your progress, seek feedback from your team and customers, and be prepared to adapt your strategies as needed. In doing so, you'll create a restaurant that not only serves great food but also nourishes a culture of respect, creativity, and belonging for all who walk through its doors.

Measuring Cultural Impact

The restaurant industry thrives on the energy and dedication of its people, making the cultivation of a positive workplace culture not just a nice-to-have, but an essential ingredient for success. As you embark on the journey of cultural transformation within your establishment, it's crucial to have a clear understanding of how these changes are impacting your team and your business. Measuring the impact of cultural initiatives provides valuable insights that can guide future decisions and help refine your approach to creating a supportive and inclusive environment.

One of the most effective tools for assessing cultural impact is the employee engagement survey. This comprehensive questionnaire goes into various aspects of the work experience, including job satisfaction, communication effectiveness, and alignment with company values. When designing your survey, it's important to craft questions that specifically address the cultural changes you've implemented. For instance, if you've introduced new recognition programs, ask employees how these initiatives have affected their sense of value within the organization. By conducting these surveys at regular intervals, such as quarterly or bi-annually, you can track trends over time and identify areas where your cultural initiatives are gaining traction or falling short.

Another powerful method for measuring cultural impact is through the analysis of key performance indicators (KPIs) that are directly influenced by workplace culture. In the restaurant industry, these might include metrics such as employee turnover rates, customer satisfaction scores, and even financial performance indicators like covers per labor hour or sales per labor hour. By closely monitoring these KPIs before and after implementing cultural changes, you can draw correlations between your initiatives and tangible business outcomes. For example, if you've focused on fostering a more supportive team environment, you might observe a decrease in turnover rates and an increase in customer satisfaction scores as employees become more engaged and motivated in their roles.

Focus groups and one-on-one interviews provide a more qualitative approach to assessing cultural impact. These intimate settings allow for deeper discussions about the nuances of workplace culture that might not be captured in surveys or KPIs. When conducting these sessions, create an atmosphere of trust and openness where employees feel comfortable sharing their honest thoughts and experiences. Ask probing questions about how specific cultural initiatives have affected their day-to-day work life, their relationships with colleagues, and their overall job satisfaction. These conversations can uncover valuable insights and personal anecdotes that bring your cultural data to life, providing context and depth to the numbers you've gathered through other methods.

As you collect and analyze this wealth of cultural data, it's essential to approach the process with an open mind and a willingness to make adjustments based on your findings. If certain initiatives aren't resonating with your team or producing the desired results, don't be afraid to pivot or try new approaches. The key is to maintain a dialogue with your employees throughout the process, sharing the insights you've gained and involving them in brainstorming solutions to any challenges that arise. This collaborative approach not only leads to more effective cultural strategies but also reinforces the inclusive environment you're striving to create.

Remember that measuring cultural impact is not a one-time event but an ongoing process that should be integrated into your regular business practices. By consistently gathering and analyzing data on your cultural initiatives, you can create a feedback loop that drives continuous improvement. This iterative approach allows you to fine-tune your strategies over time, ensuring that your efforts to build a supportive and inclusive workplace culture remain relevant and effective as your business evolves.

As you implement these measurement tools and strategies, it's crucial to communicate the results transparently with your team. Share both the successes and the areas for improvement and involve your staff in developing action plans based on the insights gained. This level of transparency and collaboration not only reinforces your commitment to cultural growth but also empowers your employees to take ownership of the process, further strengthening the positive culture you're working to build.

In the fast-paced and often challenging environment of the restaurant industry, the impact of a strong, supportive culture cannot be overstated. By diligently measuring and adjusting your cultural initiatives, you're not just improving workplace satisfaction – you're laying the foundation for long-term success, reduced turnover, and a reputation as an employer of choice in your community. The investment of time and resources in this process will pay dividends in the form of a more engaged, productive, and loyal workforce, ultimately leading to a more successful and resilient business in an industry known for its high pressures and tight margins.

Recap and Actionable Steps

Building a supportive and inclusive workplace culture in the restaurant industry isn't just a feel-good initiative; it's a critical component of success in an increasingly competitive market. Throughout this chapter, we've explored various aspects of cultivating a positive work environment, from defining your cultural vision to implementing changes and measuring their impact. Now, let's distill these insights into a comprehensive summary and provide you with concrete, actionable steps to transform your restaurant's culture.

At its core, a supportive culture in the restaurant industry revolves around creating an environment where every team member feels valued, heard, and empowered to contribute their best. This type of culture doesn't happen by accident; it requires intentional effort, consistent reinforcement, and a genuine commitment from leadership. When done right, it can significantly reduce turnover rates, boost employee satisfaction, and ultimately lead to improved customer experiences and increased profitability.

One of the key takeaways from our discussion is the importance of clearly defining and articulating your desired culture. This involves more than just crafting a mission statement or listing core values on a wall. It requires a deep understanding of your restaurant's identity, goals, and the unique needs of your team. Your cultural vision should align with your broader business objectives while also resonating with the diverse individuals who make up your workforce.

Implementing cultural change is often the most challenging part of the process. It demands patience, persistence, and a willingness to lead by example. Gradual changes, coupled with open communication and employee involvement, tend to be more effective than sweeping overhauls. Remember, your team members are not just passive recipients of culture; they are active participants in shaping and maintaining it. By engaging them in the change process, you not only gain valuable insights but also foster a sense of ownership and commitment to the new cultural norms.

Inclusivity and diversity are non-negotiable elements of a supportive workplace culture in today's restaurant industry. An inclusive environment goes beyond mere tolerance; it actively celebrates differences and leverages diverse perspectives to drive innovation and creativity. This approach not only enhances team dynamics but also helps your restaurant better serve a diverse customer base, potentially opening up new market opportunities.

Measuring the impact of your cultural initiatives is crucial for ongoing refinement and success. While culture can seem intangible, there are concrete metrics you can track, such as employee satisfaction scores, turnover rates, and even customer feedback. Regular assessments allow you to identify areas of improvement and adjust your strategies, accordingly, ensuring that your cultural efforts remain aligned with your business goals and team needs.

Now, let's break down the process of building a supportive and inclusive culture into actionable steps you can start implementing in your restaurant today:

• Conduct a cultural audit: Begin by assessing your current workplace culture. Gather feedback from employees at all levels through anonymous surveys, focus groups, and one-on-one interviews. Pay attention to both positive aspects and areas of concern. • Define your cultural vision: Based on the audit results and your business goals, clearly articulate the culture you want to create. Be specific about behaviors, values, and attitudes that will characterize your ideal work environment. • Develop a cultural roadmap: Create a detailed plan for implementing cultural changes. Break it down into short-term and long-term goals, with specific milestones and timelines. • Communicate the vision: Share your cultural vision and roadmap with all team members. Use multiple channels (meetings, emails, posters) to ensure the message reaches everyone. • Lead by example: As a leader, embody the cultural values you want to see. Your actions will set the tone for the entire organization. • Provide cultural training: Offer workshops and training sessions to help employees understand and embrace the new cultural norms. Focus on practical skills like effective communication, conflict resolution, and inclusive behaviors. • Revise policies and procedures: Ensure that your operational policies align with your cultural vision.

This might involve updating hiring practices, performance evaluations, or conflict resolution procedures. • Create inclusive spaces: Make physical changes to your restaurant to promote inclusivity. This could include gender-neutral restrooms, prayer or meditation rooms, or communal spaces that encourage interaction. • Implement a mentorship program: Pair newer employees with experienced team members to foster a sense of belonging and support professional growth. • Celebrate diversity: Organize events and initiatives that highlight and celebrate the diverse backgrounds of your team members. This could include cultural potlucks, heritage month celebrations, or spotlighting employee stories. • Establish feedback mechanisms: Create channels for ongoing feedback about the workplace culture. This could be a suggestion box, regular pulse surveys, or an open-door policy with management. • Recognize and reward cultural champions: Identify and publicly acknowledge employees who exemplify the desired cultural values. This reinforces positive behaviors and motivates others. • Measure and adjust: Regularly assess the impact of your cultural initiatives using both quantitative (turnover rates, productivity metrics) and qualitative (employee satisfaction, customer feedback) measures. Use these insights to refine your approach. • Foster cross-departmental collaboration: Encourage interaction between different teams or shifts to break down silos and promote a unified culture across the entire restaurant. • Invest in employee well-being: Implement programs that support the holistic well-being of your staff, such as flexible scheduling, mental health resources, or wellness initiatives. • Create a culture committee: Form a diverse group of employees to help drive and maintain cultural initiatives. This promotes ownership and ensures diverse perspectives are considered in decision-making.

Remember, building a supportive and inclusive workplace culture is an ongoing process, not a one-time event. It requires consistent effort, adaptability, and a genuine commitment to the well-being of your team. By following these steps and remaining dedicated to your cultural vision, you can create a work environment that not only retains top talent but also drives your restaurant's success in an ever-evolving industry landscape.

Innovative Strategies for the Restaurant Industry

Problem Introduction

The restaurant industry has long been plagued by a set of practices that, while once effective, now struggle to meet the unique demands of this fast-paced, high-turnover sector. These traditional approaches, often borrowed from corporate environments, fail to address the specific challenges faced by restaurants, leaving owners and managers grappling with a constant cycle of recruitment, training, and retention issues that drain resources and hinder growth. As costs continue to rise and profit margins narrow, the need for innovative strategies tailored to the restaurant industry has never been more critical.

Consider the typical hiring process in a restaurant: a hurried interview, a quick review of experience, and a decision often based more on immediate need than long-term fit. This approach, while seemingly efficient, often results in a revolving door of employees, each departure representing a significant cost in terms of time, money, and team morale. The limitations of these outdated practices extend beyond recruitment, permeating every aspect of people management in restaurants, from performance evaluations that fail to capture the nuances of service roles to training programs that barely scratch the surface of what's needed for success in a dynamic dining environment.

The restaurant industry's unique characteristics demand a fresh perspective on strategies. The high-stress nature of kitchen work, the unpredictable ebb and flow of customer traffic, and the necessity for seamless teamwork under pressure create a work environment unlike any other. Traditional practices, designed for more stable and predictable industries, often fall short in addressing these challenges. They fail to account for the importance of adaptability, the value of personality fit in customer-facing roles, and the critical need for rapid skill development in an industry where trends can shift overnight.

The restaurant sector's notoriously thin profit margins leave little room for error in staffing decisions. Each hire represents a significant investment, and the cost of a bad fit extends far beyond the individual, potentially impacting customer satisfaction, team dynamics, and ultimately, the bottom line. The industry's high turnover rate, often exceeding 70% annually, is not just a symptom of these outdated practices but a clear indication that a fundamental shift in approach is necessary. This revolving door of talent creates a constant drain on resources, forcing managers to focus on filling gaps rather than developing and nurturing a skilled, loyal workforce.

The need for innovative strategies in the restaurant industry is further underscored by the changing expectations of the workforce itself. Today's restaurant employees, particularly those from younger generations, seek more than just a paycheck. They desire growth opportunities, work-life balance, and a sense of purpose in their careers. Traditional practices, often focused solely on compliance and basic needs, fail to address these deeper motivations, leading to disengagement and, ultimately, turnover. By reimagining strategies to align with these evolving expectations, restaurants can not only reduce turnover but also create a more engaged, productive, and loyal workforce.

Addressing these challenges requires a paradigm shift in how restaurants approach people. It calls for strategies that are as dynamic and adaptable as the industry itself, capable of meeting both the immediate operational needs and the long-term goals of growth and sustainability. This shift involves rethinking every aspect of, from how talent is attracted and selected to how performance is measured and rewarded. It requires a holistic approach that considers the unique culture of each restaurant, the specific skills needed for success in different roles, and the motivations that drive employee satisfaction and retention in this high-pressure environment.

The path forward lies in developing strategies that are specifically tailored to the restaurant industry's unique challenges and opportunities. This means moving beyond one-size-fits-all solutions and embracing innovative approaches that reflect the realities of restaurant work. It involves leveraging technology to streamline processes, utilizing data to make more informed decisions, and creating flexible systems that can adapt to the ever-changing landscape of the dining world. By doing so, restaurants can transform from a necessary administrative function into a strategic asset that drives business success and creates a competitive advantage in a crowded market.

Recruitment and Selection Innovations

The restaurant industry faces unique challenges when it comes to attracting and retaining top talent. With high turnover rates and fierce competition for skilled workers, traditional recruitment methods often fall short. To stay ahead in this dynamic environment, restaurant owners and managers must embrace innovative approaches to talent acquisition that not only fill positions but also ensure a better fit between employees and the organization's culture.

One of the most effective ways to revolutionize your recruitment process is by leveraging the power of social media platforms. These digital spaces offer unprecedented access to a vast pool of potential candidates, many of whom may not be actively job hunting but could be enticed by the right opportunity. Platforms like Instagram and TikTok, with their visual-centric formats, provide an ideal stage to showcase your restaurant's unique atmosphere, team camaraderie, and behind-the-scenes operations. By creating engaging content that highlights your establishment's culture and values, you can attract individuals who resonate with your brand ethos, increasing the likelihood of finding candidates who will thrive in your environment.

To maximize the impact of your social media recruitment efforts, consider implementing a strategic content calendar that balances promotional job postings with authentic glimpses into your restaurant's daily life. This could include short videos of your chefs preparing signature dishes, staff testimonials sharing their experiences, or even live Q&A sessions where potential applicants can interact directly with your team. By fostering this level of transparency and engagement, you not only attract more candidates but also provide them with a realistic preview of what it's like to work in your establishment, helping to set clear expectations from the outset.

While social media can cast a wide net, it's equally important to refine your selection process to identify the most promising candidates efficiently. One innovative approach gaining traction in the restaurant industry is the use of gamified assessments. These interactive evaluations simulate real-world scenarios that employees might encounter on the job, allowing you to assess their problem-solving skills, customer service aptitude, and ability to work under pressure in a more engaging and revealing manner than traditional interviews alone.

For example, you could design a virtual simulation where candidates must manage a busy dinner service, handling everything from seating arrangements to resolving customer complaints. This not only provides valuable insights into their capabilities but also gives candidates a taste of the challenges they'll face, helping them self-select out if they feel the role isn't a good fit. By incorporating these gamified elements into your selection process, you can make more informed hiring decisions while simultaneously reducing the likelihood of early turnover due to misaligned expectations.

Another innovative recruitment strategy that's proving effective in the restaurant industry is the implementation of employee referral programs with a twist. Instead of offering a one-time bonus for successful referrals, consider creating a tiered reward system that incentivizes not just the initial referral but also the long-term success of the new hire. This approach encourages your current staff to think critically about who they recommend, as their rewards are tied to the referred employee's performance and tenure.

For instance, you could structure a program where the referring employee receives an initial bonus when their referral is hired, another bonus when the new hire completes their probationary period, and additional rewards at the six-month and one-year marks. This not only motivates your existing team to actively participate in the recruitment process but also fosters a sense of investment in the success of new team members, promoting a more cohesive and supportive work environment.

To further enhance your selection process, consider implementing personality assessments tailored specifically to the restaurant industry. While general personality tests can provide some insights, tools designed with the unique demands of hospitality in mind can offer more relevant and actionable data. These assessments can help you identify candidates who possess the traits most conducive to success in your particular restaurant environment, such as adaptability, empathy, and the ability to thrive in high-pressure situations.

When utilizing these assessments, it's crucial to view them as one piece of the puzzle rather than a definitive measure of a candidate's potential. Combine the results with structured interviews, practical skills tests, and trial shifts to build a comprehensive picture of each applicant. This multi-faceted approach not only helps you make more informed hiring decisions but also demonstrates to candidates that you're invested in finding the right fit for both parties, setting the stage for a more committed and engaged workforce.

As you implement these innovative recruitment and selection strategies, remember that the process doesn't end with a job offer. The onboarding experience plays a critical role in setting new hires up for success and reducing early turnover. Consider developing a comprehensive digital onboarding platform that new employees can access before their first day. This platform could include virtual tours of the restaurant, introductions to key team members, detailed explanations of policies and procedures, and interactive training modules on essential skills and safety protocols.

By providing this information upfront, you allow new hires to familiarize themselves with your restaurant's operations and culture at their own pace, reducing anxiety and increasing their readiness to hit the ground running. Additionally, this digital approach allows you to track each new employee's progress through the onboarding process, identifying areas where they may need additional support or training before they even step foot in the kitchen or dining room.

Employee Engagement and Motivation

The restaurant industry thrives on the energy and dedication of its workforce. In an environment where customer satisfaction hinges on the quality of service provided, employee engagement and motivation become paramount. Traditional methods of keeping staff invested in their roles often fall short in the fast-paced, high-pressure world of food service. It's time to explore creative approaches that resonate with the unique challenges and opportunities present in restaurants, cafes, and other culinary establishments.

At the heart of employee engagement lies the concept of connection – to the job, to colleagues, and to the overall mission of the establishment. In a restaurant setting, this connection can be fostered through immersive training programs that go beyond basic skills. Consider implementing a "Chef for a Day" program where front-of-house staff spend time in the kitchen, learning about ingredient selection, food preparation, and plating techniques. This not only broadens their knowledge base but also instills a deeper appreciation for the culinary process, enabling them to speak more passionately about menu items to customers.

Motivation in the restaurant industry often stems from a sense of progression and mastery. Develop a tiered skill system where employees can earn certifications in various aspects of restaurant operations. This could include advanced wine knowledge, mixology expertise, or even management skills. As staff members progress through these tiers, they not only enhance their value to the establishment but also build a sense of personal accomplishment. Tie these achievements to tangible rewards such as pay increases, choice of shifts, or opportunities to create special menu items.

Recognition plays a crucial role in maintaining high levels of motivation. Move beyond the traditional "Employee of the Month" plaque and implement a real-time feedback system. Utilize a digital platform where managers, colleagues, and even customers can leave instant praise for exceptional service or teamwork. Display these kudos on screens in staff areas, creating a constant stream of positive reinforcement. This immediate acknowledgment of good work taps into the desire for instant gratification that many in the younger workforce crave.

In an industry known for its long and often unsociable hours, work-life balance can be a significant motivator. Explore flexible scheduling options that allow employees to have more control over their work hours. Implement a self-scheduling system where staff can trade shifts or pick up extra hours based on their personal needs and preferences. This level of autonomy can greatly reduce stress and increase job satisfaction, leading to higher retention rates and a more stable workforce.

Financial incentives remain a powerful motivational tool, but they need to be structured in a way that aligns with the ebb and flow of restaurant operations. Consider implementing a profit-sharing program that distributes a percentage of monthly or quarterly profits among staff. This not only provides additional income but also fosters a sense of ownership and encourages employees to contribute to the overall success of the establishment. Be transparent about how these bonuses are calculated, and provide regular updates on the restaurant's financial performance to keep everyone invested in the bigger picture.

Creating a culture of continuous learning and development is essential for long-term engagement. Partner with local culinary schools or industry experts to offer regular workshops and masterclasses. These could cover a wide range of topics from advanced service techniques to the latest food trends. By investing in your employees' professional growth, you demonstrate a commitment to their future, whether that's within your establishment or in the broader culinary world.

Team building in a restaurant setting should go beyond the occasional staff outing. Organize regular "family meals" where staff from all areas of the restaurant come together to share a meal before service. Use this time not just for eating but for open discussions about menu changes, customer feedback, and ideas for improvement. This practice builds camaraderie, breaks down barriers between front and back of house, and gives everyone a voice in the operation of the restaurant.

Aligning employee goals with organizational objectives is crucial for sustained motivation. Implement a goal-setting program where each staff member, from dishwashers to managers, sets personal and professional objectives that tie into the restaurant's overall mission. These could range from improving specific skills to contributing to customer satisfaction scores. Regular check-ins to discuss progress on these goals keep employees focused and engaged, while also providing opportunities for managers to offer support and resources.

In an industry where physical and emotional demands can be high, prioritizing employee well-being is a powerful engagement strategy. Develop a comprehensive wellness program that addresses the specific health challenges faced by restaurant workers. This could include partnerships with local gyms, access to mental health resources, and education on proper nutrition and sleep habits. By showing that you care about your employees' health and happiness beyond their work performance, you foster a deeper sense of loyalty and commitment.

Ultimately, the most effective employee engagement and motivation strategies in the restaurant industry are those that recognize and celebrate the unique passion and creativity that draws people to this field. By creating an environment where staff feel valued, supported, and inspired, you not only improve the day-to-day operations of your establishment but also contribute to the elevation of the industry as a whole. As you implement these strategies, remember that engagement is an ongoing process, requiring constant attention and adaptation to the evolving needs of your workforce and the ever-changing landscape of the culinary world.

Performance Management Enhancements

Performance management in the restaurant industry has long been a challenge, often relying on outdated methods that fail to capture the nuances of this dynamic environment. Traditional annual reviews and rigid metrics simply don't cut it in a sector where customer satisfaction, teamwork, and adaptability are paramount. It's time to revolutionize how we evaluate and support our staff, moving away from punitive measures and towards a system that fosters growth, engagement, and ultimately, better service.

The first step in enhancing performance management is to recognize that the restaurant industry operates on a different rhythm than most. The fast-paced, customer-facing nature of the work demands a more frequent and flexible approach to evaluation. Instead of relying on annual or semi-annual reviews, consider implementing a system of ongoing feedback and coaching. This could take the form of weekly or bi-weekly check-ins between managers and staff, providing opportunities for real-time guidance and recognition. These regular touchpoints allow for immediate course correction when needed and timely praise when deserved, creating a culture of continuous improvement rather than periodic judgment.

When it comes to metrics, it's crucial to move beyond the traditional focus on sales figures or customer complaints. While these are important, they don't tell the whole story of an employee's contribution to the restaurant's success. Consider incorporating metrics that reflect the multifaceted nature of restaurant work. For front-of-house staff, this might include measures of teamwork, such as how often they assist colleagues during busy periods or their ability to smoothly hand off tables. For kitchen staff, metrics could include consistency in food preparation, adherence to health and safety standards, and ability to adapt to menu changes or special requests. By broadening the scope of what we measure, we create a more holistic view of performance that aligns with the realities of restaurant work.

Another key enhancement is the integration of peer feedback into the performance management process. In a restaurant setting, colleagues often have the best insight into each other's performance, particularly during high-pressure situations. Implementing a system where staff can provide constructive feedback on their peers not only offers a more comprehensive view of an employee's performance but also fosters a sense of shared responsibility for the team's success. This could be done through anonymous surveys or structured peer review sessions, ensuring that feedback is both honest and constructive. It's important, however, to provide training on how to give and receive feedback effectively to prevent this process from becoming a source of conflict.

Technology can play a significant role in modernizing performance management in restaurants. Consider implementing digital platforms that allow for easy tracking of key performance indicators, scheduling of check-ins, and documentation of feedback. These tools can provide valuable data insights, helping managers identify trends and patterns in performance across their team. For instance, a digital system could highlight which shifts or sections tend to result in higher customer satisfaction scores, allowing for more informed staffing decisions. In addition, such platforms can facilitate more transparent communication about performance expectations and progress, empowering employees to take ownership of their professional development.

One often overlooked aspect of performance management in restaurants is the role of customer feedback. While many establishments already collect customer reviews, few effectively integrate this information into their performance management systems. Developing a method to systematically analyze and incorporate customer feedback into employee evaluations can provide valuable insights. This could involve creating a scoring system based on specific aspects of service mentioned in reviews or implementing a process for managers to regularly discuss positive customer comments with staff. By directly linking customer experiences to performance evaluations, we reinforce the connection between individual actions and overall restaurant success.

It's crucial to align performance management with career development opportunities. In an industry known for high turnover, showing employees a clear path for growth can significantly improve retention and motivation. This might involve creating skill matrices that outline the competencies needed for various roles within the restaurant, from line cook to sous chef, or from server to floor manager. Regular performance discussions should include conversations about an employee's career aspirations and concrete steps they can take to progress. By tying performance management to professional development, we transform it from a potentially stressful evaluation into an opportunity for growth and advancement.

Finally, consider implementing a recognition and rewards system that goes beyond traditional employee-of-the-month programs. This could involve on-the-spot recognition for exceptional service, team-based rewards for achieving collective goals, or a points system that allows employees to earn perks or benefits based on their performance over time. The key is to make recognition frequent, specific, and meaningful. Celebrate not just the big wins but also the small, everyday actions that contribute to a positive dining experience. By creating a culture of appreciation and recognition, we reinforce the behaviors and attitudes that drive success in the restaurant industry.

Enhancing performance management in restaurants requires a shift in mindset from evaluation to development, from periodic reviews to ongoing coaching, and from rigid metrics to holistic assessments. By implementing these innovative approaches, restaurant owners and managers can create a more engaged, skilled, and motivated workforce. This not only improves the dining experience for customers but also builds a more stable and successful business in an industry known for its challenges. Remember, effective performance management is not about finding fault; it's about nurturing talent and creating an environment where every team member can thrive.

Handling Challenges

The restaurant industry is rife with unique challenges that can make or break a business. From high turnover rates to scheduling conflicts, these issues can significantly impact the bottom line and overall workplace atmosphere. One of the most prevalent challenges is managing employee burnout, a pervasive problem in an industry known for its long hours and high-stress environment. This burnout often leads to decreased productivity, increased absenteeism, and ultimately, staff turnover. To combat this, some innovative restaurants have implemented mandatory break periods during shifts, even in the midst of busy service times, ensuring that staff have a chance to recharge and refocus.

Another common hurdle in the restaurant world is the struggle to maintain consistent communication across different shifts and departments. With the fast-paced nature of service and the often-fragmented schedule of restaurant work, important information can easily fall through the cracks, leading to misunderstandings and operational inefficiencies. To address this, forward-thinking establishments have begun utilizing digital platforms that allow for real-time updates and communication between all staff members, regardless of their working hours. These platforms can include features such as shift notes, inventory updates, and even customer feedback, ensuring that everyone from the head chef to the newest busser is on the same page.

The issue of fair and equitable pay is another significant challenge that plagues many restaurants. The tipping system, while traditional, can lead to vast discrepancies in earnings between front-of-house and back-of-house staff, often causing tension and resentment among team members. Some innovative restaurants have tackled this by implementing a pooled tipping system or even eliminating tipping altogether in favor of a service charge that is distributed more evenly among all staff. This approach not only helps to create a more harmonious work environment but can also lead to improved overall service as staff members are incentivized to work together as a cohesive unit rather than competing for individual tips.

Training and development present another significant challenge in the restaurant industry. With high turnover rates, it can be tempting for management to provide only minimal training to new hires, focusing on getting them onto the floor as quickly as possible. However, this short-sighted approach often leads to poor service, mistakes, and ultimately, dissatisfied customers. Progressive restaurants are addressing this by implementing comprehensive training programs that go beyond basic job duties. These programs often include cross-training across different roles, wine and food pairing education, and even leadership development for promising staff members. By investing in their employees' growth and development, these restaurants are not only improving their service quality but also increasing employee engagement and retention.

The challenge of scheduling in the restaurant industry cannot be overstated. With fluctuating customer demand, special events, and the personal lives of staff to consider, creating a fair and efficient schedule can feel like solving a complex puzzle. Some innovative restaurants have turned to AI-powered scheduling software to help manage this task. These systems can take into account factors such as sales forecasts, employee availability, and even local events to create optimal schedules. They often include features that allow staff to easily swap shifts or request time off, reducing the administrative burden on management and improving work-life balance for employees.

Diversity and inclusion represent another critical challenge in the restaurant industry. Many establishments struggle to create truly inclusive environments that celebrate diversity in all its forms. Progressive restaurants are addressing this by implementing blind hiring practices to reduce unconscious bias, offering diversity and inclusion training for all staff members, and actively seeking out diverse candidates for leadership positions. Some have even gone as far as to create mentorship programs specifically designed to support and elevate underrepresented groups within their organization. These efforts not only create a more equitable workplace but can also lead to increased creativity, improved problem-solving, and a more diverse customer base.

The issue of harassment and misconduct is unfortunately all too common in the restaurant industry. Creating a safe and respectful work environment is not only a moral imperative but also a critical factor in employee retention and overall business success. Forward-thinking restaurants are tackling this challenge head-on by implementing clear, zero-tolerance policies, providing regular training on appropriate workplace behavior, and establishing confidential reporting systems. Some have even partnered with third-party organizations to conduct regular climate surveys and provide additional support and resources to their staff. By prioritizing the safety and well-being of all employees, these restaurants are creating environments where everyone can thrive professionally.

Addressing these challenges requires a commitment to innovation and a willingness to break away from traditional industry norms. By implementing creative solutions and prioritizing the well-being of their staff, restaurants can create more positive, productive, and profitable work environments. The key lies in recognizing that employees are not just cogs in a machine, but valuable assets whose satisfaction and engagement directly correlate to the success of the business. As the industry continues to evolve, those establishments that can effectively navigate these challenges will be best positioned to attract and retain top talent, provide exceptional customer experiences, and ultimately thrive in an increasingly competitive marketplace.

Recap and Actionable Steps

Innovative strategies are the lifeblood of a thriving restaurant business, transforming the way we approach talent management and employee satisfaction in an industry known for its high turnover rates and unique challenges. By embracing these forward-thinking approaches, restaurant owners and managers can create a work environment that not only attracts top talent but also nurtures and retains it, ultimately leading to improved operational efficiency, customer satisfaction, and profitability. The key lies in understanding that traditional practices often fall short in addressing the specific needs of the restaurant industry, necessitating a paradigm shift in how we view and implement people management.

At the heart of these innovative strategies is a focus on personalized recruitment and selection processes that go beyond the standard resume review and interview. By leveraging social media platforms and industry-specific job boards, restaurants can cast a wider net and connect with potential employees who are genuinely passionate about the culinary world. This approach not only increases the chances of finding the right fit but also helps in building a team that aligns with the restaurant's culture and values. Implementing creative assessment methods, such as hands-on trials or team-based challenges, can provide a more accurate picture of a candidate's skills and compatibility with the fast-paced restaurant environment.

Employee engagement and motivation take on new dimensions with innovative strategies tailored to the restaurant industry. Recognizing that monetary incentives alone may not be sufficient in retaining top talent, forward-thinking establishments are implementing programs that offer growth opportunities, work-life balance, and a sense of belonging. This could include cross-training initiatives that allow staff to explore different roles within the restaurant, flexible scheduling options that accommodate personal commitments, and team-building activities that foster camaraderie among employees. By aligning individual aspirations with organizational goals, restaurants can create a workforce that is not only motivated but also invested in the long-term success of the business.

Performance management in the restaurant industry is undergoing a significant transformation, moving away from rigid annual reviews to more frequent, constructive feedback sessions. This shift acknowledges the dynamic nature of restaurant operations and the need for real-time performance improvements. Innovative metrics that go beyond traditional sales figures are being introduced, such as customer satisfaction scores, teamwork evaluations, and adherence to food safety standards. By providing regular, actionable feedback and recognizing achievements promptly, restaurants can create a culture of continuous improvement and excellence.

Addressing challenges in the restaurant industry requires a proactive and creative approach. From managing diverse teams to handling peak-hour stress, innovative solutions are emerging to tackle these persistent issues. For instance, some establishments are implementing mentorship programs to support new hires, reducing turnover rates and fostering a supportive work environment. Others are utilizing technology to streamline scheduling processes, minimizing conflicts and ensuring fair distribution of shifts. By addressing these challenges head-on with innovative solutions, restaurants can create a more stable and harmonious work environment.

To implement these innovative strategies effectively in your restaurant, consider the following actionable steps:

Conduct a comprehensive audit of your current practices, identifying areas that need improvement or modernization.

Develop a tailored recruitment strategy that leverages social media and industry-specific platforms to attract passionate and skilled candidates.

Implement a structured onboarding program that goes beyond basic training, incorporating elements of company culture and long-term career development.

Establish a regular feedback system that encourages open communication between management and staff, fostering a culture of continuous improvement.

Create a recognition program that celebrates both individual and team achievements, reinforcing positive behaviors and boosting morale.

Invest in technology solutions that can streamline processes, such as scheduling software or digital performance tracking tools.

Develop cross-training opportunities that allow employees to expand their skills and explore different roles within the restaurant.

Implement flexible scheduling options that balance business needs with employee preferences, promoting work-life balance.

Establish clear career progression paths within your organization, showing employees potential growth opportunities.

Regularly review and adjust your strategies based on employee feedback and industry trends to ensure continued effectiveness.

By embracing these innovative strategies and implementing them thoughtfully, restaurant owners and managers can create a work environment that not only attracts top talent but also nurtures and retains it. This approach leads to a more stable, motivated, and high-performing team, which in turn translates to improved customer experiences and business success. Remember, the key to effective management in the restaurant industry lies in continuously adapting and refining your strategies to meet the evolving needs of your workforce and the dynamic nature of the culinary world.

Adopting a Data-Driven Approach to Restaurant Management

Problem Introduction

In today's fast-paced restaurant industry, data has become the secret ingredient that separates thriving establishments from those struggling to keep their doors open. Gone are the days when gut feelings and intuition alone could guide a restaurant to success. The increasing importance of data in managing restaurants effectively cannot be overstated, as it provides invaluable insights into every aspect of operations, from inventory management and menu optimization to staff scheduling and customer preferences. However, despite its undeniable value, many restaurant owners and managers find themselves hesitant to fully embrace a data-driven approach, often feeling overwhelmed by the sheer volume of information available or unsure of how to harness its power effectively.

The restaurant industry, known for its razor-thin profit margins and high-pressure environment, faces unique challenges when it comes to adopting data-driven practices. One of the most common obstacles is the misconception that implementing data analytics requires a significant investment in expensive technology or specialized staff. This belief often leads smaller establishments to shy away from data-driven strategies, mistakenly assuming they're reserved for large chains with deep pockets. In reality, even modest data collection and analysis efforts can yield substantial benefits for restaurants of all sizes, from neighborhood cafes to upscale dining destinations.

Another hurdle many restaurant professionals encounter is the fear of change. The industry has long relied on traditional methods and time-honored practices passed down through generations. The idea of disrupting these established routines with data-driven decision-making can be daunting, especially for seasoned veterans who have built their careers on instinct and experience. This resistance to change often stems from a lack of understanding about how data can complement, rather than replace, the human element in restaurant management. It's crucial to recognize that data is a tool to enhance decision-making, not a substitute for the passion, creativity, and personal touch that are the hallmarks of successful restaurants.

The sheer volume of data available in modern restaurant operations can be overwhelming, leading to analysis paralysis. From point-of-sale systems and reservation platforms to social media feedback and online reviews, restaurants have access to an unprecedented amount of information about their business and customers. Without a clear strategy for collecting, organizing, and interpreting this data, many managers find themselves drowning in numbers, unable to extract meaningful insights or translate them into actionable strategies. This information overload can be particularly challenging for small to medium-sized restaurants that lack dedicated data analysts or sophisticated data management systems.

Perhaps the most significant barrier to adopting a data-driven approach is the perceived disconnect between data analysis and the day-to-day realities of running a restaurant. In an industry where success is often measured by the smiles on diners' faces and the energy of a bustling dining room, the idea of poring over spreadsheets and charts can seem at odds with the hospitality-focused nature of the business. Bridging this gap requires a shift in perspective, recognizing that data-driven insights can actually enhance the guest experience by allowing restaurants to tailor their offerings, improve service efficiency, and anticipate customer needs with greater accuracy.

The high turnover rate in the restaurant industry, a perennial challenge for owners and managers, also complicates the adoption of data-driven practices. With staff constantly coming and going, it can be difficult to maintain consistency in data collection and analysis processes. Training new employees on the importance of data and how to use it effectively becomes an ongoing task, often taking a back seat to more immediate concerns like food preparation and customer service. This instability can lead to gaps in data collection, inconsistencies in reporting, and a general lack of continuity in data-driven initiatives.

Despite these challenges, the potential benefits of embracing a data-driven approach in restaurant management are too significant to ignore. By overcoming these obstacles and integrating data analytics into their operations, restaurants can gain a competitive edge, improve efficiency, reduce costs, and ultimately enhance the dining experience for their guests. The key lies in demystifying the process, starting small, and gradually building a culture that values data as a critical tool for success in the ever-evolving landscape of the restaurant industry.

Collecting the Right Data

In the fast-paced world of restaurant management, data has become an indispensable tool for making informed decisions and staying ahead of the competition. However, with the sheer volume of information available, it's crucial to focus on collecting the right data that will truly impact your business. Identifying the most valuable data points for your restaurant is the first step in harnessing the power of data-driven management, allowing you to make strategic decisions that can significantly improve your operations, customer satisfaction, and ultimately, your bottom line.

When it comes to determining which data points are most valuable for your restaurant, it's essential to consider your specific business goals, operational challenges, and target market. For instance, if you're struggling with inventory management, focusing on data related to ingredient usage, waste, and sales trends can provide invaluable insights. On the other hand, if customer retention is a primary concern, you might want to prioritize data on customer feedback, loyalty program participation, and repeat visit frequency. By aligning your data collection efforts with your business objectives, you can ensure that the information you gather is both relevant and actionable. This is something that a large number of restaurants struggle with, and if you are one of them it is more important than ever to seek expertise.

One of the most critical data points for any restaurant is sales data. This encompasses not only overall revenue but also breaks down sales by menu item, time of day, day of the week, and even individual server performance. By analyzing this information, you can identify your best-selling items, peak hours, and top-performing staff members, allowing you to optimize your menu, staffing, and marketing strategies. Additionally, tracking sales data over time can help you spot trends, anticipate seasonal fluctuations, and make more accurate forecasts for inventory and staffing needs. Overall, the most important piece of sales data is guest count or "covers". Cover count is the most powerful piece of data that exists in our industry and understanding it could lead to game changing decisions that could change your business forever. However, this data shows up for you is fine, whether it arrives as individual guest count, group count, order count, ticket count, or any other way, understanding how many "covers" you serve is crucial.

Customer data is another goldmine of information that can significantly impact your restaurant's success. This includes basic demographic information, such as age, gender, and location, as well as more detailed insights into customer preferences, ordering habits, and feedback. By collecting and analyzing this data, you can create targeted marketing campaigns, personalize the dining experience, and address any recurring issues that may be affecting customer satisfaction. Understanding your customer base can help you make informed decisions about menu changes, pricing strategies, and even potential new locations for expansion.

Operational data is equally important for maintaining efficiency and profitability in your restaurant. This encompasses a wide range of metrics, including food and labor costs, table turnover rates, average ticket size, and kitchen production times. By closely monitoring these data points, you can identify areas for improvement, streamline processes, and reduce unnecessary expenses. For example, tracking food costs and waste can help you optimize your inventory management, while analyzing table turnover rates can inform decisions about seating arrangements and reservation policies.

Once you've identified the key data points for your restaurant, it's time to consider the methods and tools for efficient data collection. In today's digital age, there are numerous technologies available to streamline this process and ensure accuracy. Point-of-sale (POS) systems are often the cornerstone of data collection in restaurants, capturing crucial information about sales, inventory, and customer orders. Modern POS systems can integrate with other tools, such as inventory management software and customer relationship management

(CRM) platforms, to provide a comprehensive view of your restaurant's performance.

For collecting customer feedback and demographic information, consider implementing a loyalty program or customer survey system. These can be integrated with your POS or operated through a separate mobile app or website. Encourage customers to provide feedback after their dining experience by offering incentives such as discounts on future visits or entries into prize drawings. This not only helps you gather valuable data but also fosters customer engagement and loyalty.

To track operational metrics, consider investing in kitchen management software that can monitor food preparation times, ingredient usage, and waste. Employee scheduling and time-tracking tools can provide insights into labor costs and productivity. For larger restaurant groups or chains, business intelligence platforms can aggregate data from multiple locations, allowing for comprehensive analysis and benchmarking across the organization.

It's important to note that while technology can greatly facilitate data collection, it's not the only method available. Traditional techniques such as mystery shopping, manual inventory counts, and in-person customer surveys can still provide valuable insights, especially for smaller establishments or those with limited technology budgets. The key is to find a balance between automated and manual data collection methods that works best for your restaurant's specific needs and resources.

As you implement your data collection strategy, it's crucial to prioritize data security and compliance with privacy regulations. Ensure that any systems you use have robust security measures in place to protect sensitive customer and financial information. Train your staff on proper data handling procedures and be transparent with customers about how their data will be used and protected.

Remember that collecting data is just the first step in the process of data-driven management. To truly benefit from this information, you'll need to develop systems for regular analysis and interpretation of the data you collect. This might involve training key staff members in data analysis techniques or partnering with external consultants who specialize in restaurant analytics. By consistently reviewing and acting on the insights gleaned from your data, you can create a culture of continuous improvement in your restaurant, leading to increased efficiency, profitability, and customer satisfaction.

Analyzing Data for Insights

In the fast-paced world of restaurant management, raw data is like an uncut diamond - valuable, but not yet ready to shine. The real magic happens when you transform that data into actionable insights that can drive your business forward. This process of analysis is where the rubber meets the road, turning numbers and statistics into a roadmap for success in your restaurant.

The first step in analyzing your data is to establish clear objectives. What specific questions are you trying to answer? Are you looking to optimize your menu, improve staff efficiency, or increase customer satisfaction? By defining your goals upfront, you can focus your analysis on the most relevant data points and avoid getting lost in a sea of information.

Once you've set your objectives, it's time to dive into the data. Start by organizing your information into meaningful categories. For instance, you might group data related to sales, customer feedback, inventory, and staff performance. This categorization will help you identify patterns and correlations more easily. Remember, the goal isn't just to crunch numbers, but to uncover the stories they tell about your restaurant's operations.

One powerful technique for deriving insights from your data is trend analysis. By examining how various metrics change over time, you can spot emerging patterns that might not be apparent in day-to-day operations. For example, you might notice that sales of certain menu items spike during specific weather conditions or that customer wait times increase dramatically on Friday evenings. These trends can inform strategic decisions, such as adjusting your staffing levels or running targeted promotions.

Another valuable approach is comparative analysis. This involves benchmarking your performance against industry standards or your own historical data. By comparing your current metrics to past performance or industry averages, you can identify areas where you're excelling and those that need improvement. For instance, if your food costs are consistently higher than the industry average, it might be time to reevaluate your purchasing strategies or portion sizes.

As you analyze your data, pay close attention to outliers and anomalies. These unexpected data points often hold valuable insights. A sudden drop in sales on a typically busy night might indicate a problem with your marketing, while an unusually high number of positive reviews could point to a successful new menu item or exceptional staff performance. Don't dismiss these outliers; investigate them thoroughly to understand what they're telling you about your business.

One of the most powerful tools in your data analysis arsenal is segmentation. This involves breaking down your data into specific subgroups based on relevant characteristics. For example, you might segment your customer data by age, frequency of visits, or average spend. This allows you to tailor your strategies to different customer groups, potentially increasing loyalty and revenue. Similarly, segmenting your menu data by profitability, popularity, and preparation time can help you optimize your offerings for maximum efficiency and profit.

As you become more adept at analyzing your data, you'll start to see connections between different metrics that might not be immediately obvious. For instance, you might discover a correlation between staff training hours and customer satisfaction scores, or between the speed of service and the likelihood of return visits. These insights can guide your decision-making in powerful ways, helping you allocate resources more effectively and focus on the factors that truly drive your business success.

It's crucial to remember that data analysis isn't a one-time event, but an ongoing process. Regular analysis allows you to track the impact of your decisions over time and make continuous improvements. Set up a schedule for reviewing key metrics, perhaps weekly or monthly, depending on the volume of data you're dealing with. This consistent approach will help you stay on top of trends and respond quickly to changes in your business environment.

While the process of analyzing data can seem daunting, there are numerous tools available to help streamline the process. From simple spreadsheet applications to sophisticated business intelligence platforms, these tools can help you visualize your data, run complex analyses, and generate insightful reports. Invest time in learning to use these tools effectively - the payoff in terms of improved decision-making will be well worth the effort.

As you implement changes based on your data analysis, it's critical to monitor the results closely. Did that menu change really boost profits as expected? Has the new staffing schedule improved service times? By tracking the outcomes of your data-driven decisions, you can refine your analysis techniques and build confidence in your approach.

This feedback loop is essential for continuous improvement and long-term success in the competitive restaurant industry.

Remember, the goal of data analysis isn't just to generate reports or pretty charts - it's to drive real, tangible improvements in your restaurant's performance. Every insight you uncover should lead to an action plan. Whether it's tweaking your menu, adjusting your pricing strategy, or implementing a new training program, make sure your analysis translates into concrete steps that can move your business forward.

Implementing Data-Driven Decisions

Transforming raw data into actionable insights is only half the battle in the quest for data-driven restaurant management. The real challenge lies in seamlessly integrating these insights into your daily operations, ensuring that every decision, from menu planning to staff scheduling, is informed by solid data. This process requires a fundamental shift in how you approach restaurant management, moving from gut feelings and traditions to evidence-based strategies that can significantly improve your bottom line.

The first step in implementing data-driven decisions is to create a culture of data literacy within your organization. This means ensuring that everyone, from the head chef to the servers, understands the importance of data and how it can be used to improve their specific roles. Organize regular training sessions that teach your staff how to interpret key performance indicators (KPIs) relevant to their positions. For instance, servers should understand how their upselling efforts impact average check sizes, while kitchen staff should be aware of how ingredient usage data affects food costs and menu planning.

Once your team is on board with the data-driven approach, it's crucial to establish clear protocols for incorporating data insights into decision-making processes. This involves creating standardized procedures for reviewing data, identifying actionable insights, and implementing changes based on those insights. For example, you might institute a weekly meeting where managers review sales data, customer feedback, and inventory reports to make informed decisions about menu adjustments, pricing strategies, and staffing levels. By formalizing this process, you ensure that data-driven decision-making becomes a consistent and integral part of your restaurant's operations, rather than an occasional afterthought.

One of the most significant barriers to implementing data-driven decisions is the fear of change. Many restaurant owners and managers are hesitant to deviate from traditional practices, even when presented with compelling data that suggests a need for change. To overcome this resistance, start by implementing small, low-risk changes based on data insights. For instance, if your data shows that a particular menu item is consistently underperforming, try adjusting its presentation or ingredients before deciding to remove it entirely. These small wins can help build confidence in the data-driven approach and pave the way for more significant changes down the line.

Another crucial aspect of implementing data-driven decisions is ensuring that you have the right tools and systems in place to make data easily accessible and actionable. Invest in a robust point-of-sale (POS) system that integrates with other key software, such as inventory management and employee scheduling tools. This integration allows for real-time data analysis and enables you to make quick, informed decisions. For example, if your POS system is integrated with your inventory management software, you can easily identify which menu items are most profitable and adjust your purchasing and menu planning accordingly.

As you begin to implement data-driven decisions, it's essential to prioritize which areas of your restaurant will benefit most from this approach. Start by focusing on high-impact areas such as menu engineering, staff scheduling, and inventory management. These areas typically have the most significant impact on your restaurant's profitability and can yield quick wins that demonstrate the value of data-driven decision-making. For instance, use sales data and customer feedback to identify your most popular and profitable menu items, then adjust your menu layout and server recommendations to promote these items more effectively.

One often overlooked aspect of implementing data-driven decisions is the importance of communication. As you make changes based on data insights, it's crucial to clearly communicate the reasoning behind these changes to your staff. This transparency not only helps to build trust and buy-in but also empowers your employees to contribute their own insights and ideas based on the data they encounter in their daily work. Encourage a culture of open dialogue where staff members feel comfortable discussing data trends and suggesting improvements based on their observations.

Finally, remember that implementing data-driven decisions is an ongoing process, not a one-time event. Continuously monitor the outcomes of your data-driven changes and be prepared to make adjustments as needed. This iterative approach allows you to refine your strategies over time, ensuring that your restaurant stays agile and responsive to changing market conditions and customer preferences. By embracing this continuous improvement mindset, you'll be well-positioned to leverage data as a powerful tool for long-term success in the competitive restaurant industry.

Monitoring Outcomes and Adjusting Strategies

Implementing data-driven decisions in your restaurant is only the beginning of a transformative journey. The true power of this approach lies in the continuous monitoring of outcomes and the agile adjustment of strategies based on the insights gained. This iterative process forms the backbone of a successful data-driven management system, allowing you to fine-tune your operations, maximize efficiency, and stay ahead in the competitive restaurant industry.

To effectively track the impact of your data-driven changes, it's crucial to establish a robust monitoring system. This system should encompass various key performance indicators (KPIs) that align with your specific business goals and the changes you've implemented. These KPIs might include metrics such as average table turnover time, customer satisfaction scores, food waste percentages, or staff productivity levels (CPLH). The key is to select metrics that directly reflect the areas you're targeting for improvement and that provide clear, measurable data points for analysis.

Once you've identified your KPIs, the next step is to implement a systematic approach to data collection and analysis. This might involve utilizing point-of-sale (POS) systems that automatically track sales and inventory data, customer feedback platforms that gather and categorize reviews, or employee management software that monitors staff performance and scheduling efficiency. The goal is to create a seamless, automated process that provides you with real-time data, allowing you to make informed decisions quickly and effectively.

As you gather this wealth of information, it's essential to develop a structured method for analyzing and interpreting the data. This process should involve regular review sessions where you and your management team examine the collected data, identify trends, and assess the effectiveness of your implemented changes. During these sessions, look for both positive outcomes that validate your strategies and areas where the results fall short of expectations. It's crucial to approach this analysis with an open mind, ready to celebrate successes and confront challenges head-on.

When you identify positive outcomes, take the time to understand the factors contributing to this success. Was it a result of improved staff training, more efficient kitchen processes, or perhaps a menu optimization that resonated with your customers? By pinpointing the specific elements that led to success, you can replicate and amplify these strategies across other areas of your restaurant operations. This approach allows you to build on your successes, creating a cycle of continuous improvement that drives your business forward.

Conversely, when the data reveals areas where your strategies aren't yielding the desired results, it's time to pivot and adjust. This is where the true value of a data-driven approach shines through. Instead of relying on gut feelings or anecdotal evidence, you have concrete data to guide your decision-making process. Perhaps your new menu items aren't selling as well as anticipated, or your revised staffing schedule isn't improving service times as expected. In these situations, dive deeper into the data to understand the root causes of these shortfalls.

The process of adjusting strategies based on data analysis should be methodical and thoughtful. Start by formulating hypotheses about why certain approaches aren't working as planned. Then, design small-scale experiments or pilot programs to test these hypotheses. For instance, if a new menu item isn't performing well, you might experiment with different pricing strategies, adjust the item's description on the menu, or provide additional training to your staff on how to recommend and describe the dish to customers. By implementing these changes on a limited scale, you can gather more data and assess their effectiveness before rolling out broader changes.

It's important to remember that the process of monitoring outcomes and adjusting strategies is not a one-time event but an ongoing cycle. The restaurant industry is dynamic, with changing consumer preferences, emerging food trends, and evolving economic conditions. By consistently monitoring your data and being willing to adapt your strategies, you position your restaurant to not just survive but thrive in this ever-changing landscape. This agile approach allows you to stay ahead of trends, quickly address issues before they become major problems, and capitalize on opportunities as they arise.

To ensure the success of this continuous improvement cycle, it's crucial to foster a culture of data-driven decision-making throughout your organization. This means not only training your management team on how to interpret and act on data but also engaging your front-line staff in the process. Share relevant insights with your team, explain how data is informing decisions, and encourage them to contribute their own observations and ideas. By involving your entire team in this process, you create a more engaged workforce that is invested in the restaurant's success and more likely to embrace and implement data-driven changes effectively.

As you become more adept at monitoring outcomes and adjusting strategies, you'll likely find that your data needs evolve. Be prepared to refine your data collection methods, add new metrics as needed, and potentially invest in more sophisticated analytics tools. The goal is to create a flexible, scalable system that grows with your business and continues to provide valuable insights as your restaurant evolves.

Ultimately, the power of a data-driven approach lies not just in the initial implementation of changes but in the ongoing process of monitoring, learning, and adapting. By committing to this cycle of continuous improvement, you position your restaurant to not only overcome challenges but to innovate and excel in ways that set you apart from the competition. In an industry known for its tight margins and high turnover rates, this data-driven agility can be the key to long-term success and sustainability.

Recap and Actionable Steps

Data-driven management in the restaurant industry isn't just a buzzword; it's a powerful tool that can transform your business from the ground up. By harnessing the power of data, you're not just making educated guesses – you're making informed decisions based on cold, hard facts. This approach can lead to increased efficiency, improved customer satisfaction, and ultimately, a healthier bottom line. But it's not just about crunching numbers; it's about understanding what those numbers mean for your unique restaurant and how to leverage that knowledge to create tangible improvements.

One of the most significant benefits of adopting a data-driven approach is the ability to identify and address issues before they become major problems. For instance, by analyzing sales data, you might notice that a particular menu item isn't performing as well as expected. Instead of waiting for complaints or seeing a gradual decline in orders, you can proactively adjust the recipe, presentation, or pricing to boost its popularity. This kind of preemptive action can save you both money and reputation in the long run.

Data can provide invaluable insights into your staff performance and customer behavior. By tracking metrics such as server efficiency, table turnover rates, and peak hours, you can optimize your staffing schedule to ensure you're never over or understaffed. This not only improves your operational efficiency but also enhances the customer experience by reducing wait times and ensuring consistent service quality. Similarly, analyzing customer data can help you tailor your marketing efforts, create personalized experiences, and develop loyalty programs that truly resonate with your patrons.

But perhaps the most compelling argument for embracing data-driven management is its potential to significantly impact your financial performance. By closely monitoring your food costs, labor expenses, and profit margins on individual menu items, you can make strategic decisions that directly affect your profitability. For example, you might discover that a popular dish is actually costing you money due to high ingredient costs or preparation time. Armed with this information, you can either adjust the pricing, modify the recipe, or consider removing it from the menu altogether – decisions that would be much harder to make without concrete data to back them up.

Now, let's break down some actionable steps you can take to start integrating data into your management practices:

• Identify your key performance indicators (KPIs): Start by determining which metrics are most crucial for your restaurant's success. These might include food cost percentage profit contribution, labor cost percentage CPLH, SPLH, average ticket size, customer satisfaction scores, and table turnover rate. • Implement a robust point-of-sale (POS) system: Choose a POS system that not only processes transactions but also collects and organizes data on sales, inventory, and customer behavior. Many modern POS systems offer built-in analytics features that can provide valuable insights at a glance. • Train your staff on data collection: Ensure that your team understands the importance of accurate data entry and collection. This might involve training them on proper use of the POS system, as well as encouraging them to gather qualitative data through customer interactions. • Establish a regular data review process: Set aside time each week or month to review your data and look for trends or anomalies. This could involve creating a dashboard of your key metrics or generating regular reports from your POS system. • Start small and scale up: Begin by focusing on one or two key areas where you believe data can make the biggest impact. As you become more comfortable with data analysis, gradually expand your focus to other aspects of your business. • Invest in data visualization tools: Consider using software that can turn your raw data into easy-to-understand charts and graphs. This can help you quickly identify trends and communicate insights to your team. • Foster a data-driven culture: Encourage your management team and staff to make decisions based on data rather than gut feelings. Share insights and successes to demonstrate the value of this approach. • Continuously refine your data strategy: As you gain more experience with data-driven management, regularly reassess which metrics are most valuable and adjust your data collection and analysis processes accordingly. • Leverage customer feedback data: Implement a system to collect and analyze customer reviews and feedback. This qualitative data can provide valuable context to your quantitative metrics. • Use data for menu engineering: Analyze the popularity and profitability of each menu item to optimize your offerings. This might involve adjusting prices, redesigning your menu layout, or introducing new dishes based on customer preferences.

Remember, transitioning to a data-driven approach is not an overnight process. It requires commitment, patience, and a willingness to challenge long-held assumptions about your business. However, the potential rewards – increased profitability, improved operational efficiency, and enhanced customer satisfaction – make it a journey well worth embarking on. By taking these steps and consistently applying data insights to your decision-making process, you'll be well on your way to running a more successful, resilient, and forward-thinking restaurant.

Future Trends and Innovations in the Restaurant Industry

Problem Introduction

The restaurant industry stands at a pivotal crossroads, where emerging trends and groundbreaking innovations are reshaping the landscape at an unprecedented pace. These changes are not merely superficial; they're fundamentally altering how restaurants operate, interact with customers, and position themselves in an increasingly competitive market. From the integration of cutting-edge technologies to shifts in consumer expectations and the growing emphasis on sustainability, the industry is experiencing a seismic shift that demands attention and adaptation from every player in the field.

For restaurant owners, managers, and staff, understanding and embracing these changes is not just advantageous—it's essential for survival and success in the evolving culinary world. The rapid pace of innovation means that what was considered cutting-edge just a few years ago may now be outdated, potentially putting businesses that fail to keep up at a significant disadvantage. This constant evolution presents both challenges and opportunities, requiring a delicate balance between maintaining the core aspects of hospitality that have always defined the industry and incorporating new elements that can enhance the dining experience and operational efficiency.

One of the most pressing issues facing the restaurant industry today is the need to stay updated with these changes while maintaining profitability in an environment of rising costs and narrow margins. The integration of new technologies, for instance, often requires significant upfront investment, both in terms of financial resources and staff training. However, the potential long-term benefits—such as improved operational efficiency, enhanced customer experiences, and increased revenue—can far outweigh the initial costs. The key lies in making informed decisions about which innovations to adopt and how to implement them effectively within the unique context of each restaurant.

The evolving landscape is not just about adopting new technologies or practices; it's about fundamentally rethinking the restaurant business model. Traditional approaches to menu design, service delivery, and customer engagement are being challenged by new consumer behaviors and expectations. Diners are increasingly seeking personalized experiences, transparency in food sourcing and preparation, and seamless integration of technology into their dining journey. This shift requires restaurants to be more flexible and responsive than ever before, constantly reevaluating and adjusting their strategies to meet changing demands.

The sustainability movement presents another critical challenge and opportunity for the industry. As awareness of environmental issues grows, consumers are becoming more conscious of the ecological impact of their dining choices. This has led to increased demand for sustainable practices in restaurants, from sourcing local and organic ingredients to implementing waste reduction strategies and energy-efficient operations. While adapting to these expectations can be complex and potentially costly, it also opens up new avenues for differentiation and customer loyalty in a crowded market.

For those working in or managing restaurants, staying ahead of these trends requires a commitment to continuous learning and adaptation. It's no longer sufficient to excel in traditional culinary skills or management practices alone; success in the modern restaurant industry demands a broader skill set that includes technological literacy, data analysis, sustainability knowledge, and the ability to anticipate and respond to rapidly changing consumer preferences. This evolving landscape presents both exciting opportunities for innovation and significant challenges in terms of resource allocation, staff training, and strategic planning.

As we go deeper into the specific trends and innovations shaping the future of the restaurant industry, it's crucial to approach each with a critical eye, evaluating not just their potential benefits but also their practical implications for implementation. The goal is not to blindly adopt every new trend or technology that emerges, but to strategically select and integrate those that align with your restaurant's vision, enhance the dining experience for your customers, and contribute to the long-term sustainability and profitability of your business. By understanding these emerging trends and innovations, you'll be better equipped to navigate the challenges and seize the opportunities that lie ahead in this dynamic and ever-evolving industry.

Technological Advances

The restaurant industry is undergoing a technological revolution that's reshaping how we operate, serve customers, and manage our businesses. From artificial intelligence to robotics, these innovations are not just futuristic concepts but tangible tools that are already making their way into kitchens and dining rooms across the globe. As restaurant owners and managers, it's crucial to understand these technological advances and their potential impact on our operations, customer experience, and bottom line.

One of the most significant technological advancements in the restaurant industry is the implementation of sophisticated point-of-sale (POS) systems. These systems have evolved far beyond simple cash registers, becoming comprehensive management tools that can track inventory, analyze sales data, manage staff schedules, and even integrate with online ordering platforms. The beauty of modern POS systems lies in their ability to provide real-time insights into your business operations, allowing you to make data-driven decisions on the fly. For instance, you can instantly see which menu items are selling well and which are underperforming, enabling you to adjust your offerings or pricing strategies accordingly.

Artificial intelligence (AI) and machine learning are also making significant inroads in the restaurant industry, offering exciting possibilities for personalization and efficiency. AI-powered chatbots, for example, can handle customer inquiries and reservations 24/7, freeing up your staff to focus on in-person customer service. These chatbots can learn from each interaction, becoming more efficient and personalized over time. AI can analyze customer data to predict preferences and behavior, allowing you to tailor your marketing efforts and menu recommendations to individual tastes. Imagine being able to send personalized promotions to customers based on their past orders or suggesting wine pairings that align with their previously expressed preferences - this level of customization can significantly enhance the dining experience and boost customer loyalty.

Robotics is another technological frontier that's beginning to impact the restaurant industry. While the idea of robot chefs might seem like science fiction, automated cooking systems are already being used in some restaurants to ensure consistency and efficiency in food preparation. These systems can perform repetitive tasks with precision, freeing up human chefs to focus on more creative aspects of cooking. In the front of house, robot servers are being tested in some establishments, particularly in fast-food settings. While they may not replace human servers entirely, they can help during peak hours or in situations where social distancing is necessary.

The rise of mobile technology has also revolutionized how customers interact with restaurants. Mobile ordering and payment apps have become increasingly popular, allowing customers to browse menus, place orders, and pay without ever speaking to a staff member. This technology not only streamlines the ordering process but also provides valuable data on customer preferences and behaviors. As a restaurant owner or manager, embracing mobile technology can help you tap into the growing market of tech-savvy diners who value convenience and speed.

Virtual and augmented reality (VR and AR) technologies are opening up new possibilities for unique dining experiences. Some high-end restaurants are experimenting with AR menus that allow diners to see 3D representations of dishes before ordering. VR, on the other hand, can be used to create immersive dining experiences, transporting guests to exotic locations or offering behind-the-scenes looks at food preparation. While these technologies might seem out of reach for many restaurants, they represent the cutting edge of experiential dining and could become more accessible in the future.

However, with these technological advances come challenges that restaurant owners and managers must navigate. The initial investment in new technologies can be significant, and there's always a learning curve associated with implementing new systems. It's crucial to carefully evaluate which technologies align with your restaurant's needs and budget. While technology can enhance efficiency and customer experience, it's important not to lose the human touch that is so vital to the hospitality industry. The key is to use technology to augment and support your staff, not replace them entirely.

Data security is another critical concern as restaurants collect more customer information through digital platforms. Implementing robust cybersecurity measures is essential to protect your customers' data and maintain their trust. This might involve investing in secure payment systems, training staff on data protection practices, and regularly updating your digital infrastructure to guard against potential breaches.

As we look to the future, it's clear that technology will continue to play an increasingly important role in the restaurant industry. The key to success lies in striking a balance between embracing innovation and maintaining the core values of hospitality that have always defined great restaurants. By thoughtfully integrating technological advances into your operations, you can enhance efficiency, improve the customer experience, and position your restaurant for success in an increasingly digital world.

Shifts in Consumer Behavior

The restaurant industry is experiencing a seismic shift in consumer behavior, driven by a complex interplay of technological advancements, changing societal values, and evolving lifestyle preferences. These changes are not merely superficial trends but represent fundamental alterations in how people perceive, interact with, and consume food services. As restaurant owners and managers, it's crucial to not only recognize these shifts but to proactively adapt our business strategies to meet these new demands head-on.

One of the most significant changes we're witnessing is the increasing demand for convenience and speed without compromising on quality. Today's consumers, particularly millennials and Gen Z, are looking for seamless dining experiences that fit into their fast-paced lifestyles. This has led to a surge in popularity for mobile ordering, contactless payments, and delivery services. Restaurants that have embraced these technologies have seen substantial increases in customer satisfaction and loyalty. To capitalize on this trend, consider implementing a user-friendly mobile app that allows for easy ordering and payment. Ensure that your kitchen operations are streamlined to handle the influx of digital orders without sacrificing food quality or increasing wait times for in-house diners.

Another pivotal shift is the growing emphasis on health and wellness. Consumers are becoming increasingly conscious of what they put into their bodies, seeking out nutritious, balanced meals even when dining out. This doesn't necessarily mean an exclusive focus on low-calorie options, but rather a demand for transparency about ingredients, sourcing, and preparation methods. To address this, revamp your menu to include detailed nutritional information and highlight locally sourced, organic, or sustainably produced ingredients. Consider offering customizable meal options that allow diners to tailor their dishes to their dietary preferences or restrictions. This level of transparency and flexibility can significantly boost customer trust and loyalty.

The concept of dining out has also evolved beyond mere sustenance to encompass a holistic experience. Today's consumers are seeking unique, Instagram-worthy moments that they can share with their social networks. This shift towards experiential dining presents both challenges and opportunities for restaurateurs. To tap into this trend, focus on creating a distinctive atmosphere that reflects your brand identity. This could involve innovative plating techniques, interactive dining experiences, or themed events that align with your restaurant's concept. Remember, every aspect of your restaurant, from the decor to the background music, contributes to the overall dining experience and can be leveraged to create shareable moments for your guests.

Sustainability has moved from a niche concern to a mainstream expectation among consumers. Diners are increasingly making choices based on a restaurant's environmental impact and ethical practices. This extends beyond just the food on the plate to encompass packaging, waste management, and even employee treatment. To address this shift, conduct a thorough audit of your restaurant's environmental footprint and implement sustainable practices wherever possible. This could include sourcing ingredients from local farms to reduce transportation emissions, implementing a comprehensive recycling and composting program, or switching to biodegradable takeout containers. Communicate these efforts clearly to your customers, as transparency in sustainability practices can be a powerful differentiator in a competitive market.

The rise of the "foodie" culture and increased culinary knowledge among consumers has led to a demand for more diverse and authentic dining experiences. Diners are increasingly adventurous, seeking out new flavors and cuisines. This presents an opportunity for restaurants to experiment with fusion concepts or to go deep into specific regional cuisines. Consider hosting special tasting events or chef's table experiences that allow customers to explore new flavors and techniques. Regularly updating your menu with seasonal specials or limited-time offerings can keep your regulars engaged and attract new customers looking for novel dining experiences.

Lastly, the concept of value has evolved beyond just price point. While affordability remains important, consumers are increasingly willing to pay a premium for perceived value in terms of quality, experience, and alignment with their personal values. This shift necessitates a reevaluation of your pricing strategy. Rather than competing solely on price, focus on communicating the unique value proposition of your restaurant. This could be the exceptional quality of your ingredients, the skill and creativity of your chefs, or your restaurant's commitment to social or environmental causes. By clearly articulating this value, you can justify higher price points and attract customers who are willing to pay for a premium dining experience.

Adapting to these shifts in consumer behavior requires a holistic approach that touches every aspect of your restaurant operations. It's not enough to make surface-level changes; success in this evolving landscape demands a fundamental rethinking of how we approach the dining experience. By staying attuned to these trends and continuously innovating to meet changing consumer expectations, restaurants can not only survive but thrive in this new era of dining. Remember, the key is to view these changes not as challenges to be overcome, but as opportunities to differentiate your business and create lasting connections with your customers.

Sustainability Practices

Sustainability has become a cornerstone of modern restaurant operations, evolving from a mere buzzword to an essential aspect of business strategy. As environmental concerns continue to grow, customers are increasingly seeking out establishments that align with their values and demonstrate a commitment to responsible practices. This shift in consumer behavior presents both a challenge and an opportunity for restaurant owners and managers who are willing to adapt and innovate.

The concept of sustainability in the restaurant industry encompasses a wide range of practices, from sourcing ingredients to waste management and energy conservation. At its core, it's about creating a business model that minimizes negative environmental impact while maximizing positive social and economic outcomes. This holistic approach requires careful consideration of every aspect of restaurant operations, from the kitchen to the dining room and beyond.

One of the most impactful ways to implement sustainable practices is through thoughtful menu planning and ingredient sourcing. Start by conducting a thorough audit of your current suppliers and ingredients, identifying areas where you can make more sustainable choices. This might involve partnering with local farmers and producers to reduce transportation emissions and support the local economy or opting for seasonal ingredients to ensure freshness and minimize the need for energy-intensive storage and preservation methods. Consider implementing a "farm-to-table" approach, which not only promotes sustainability but also appeals to customers who value transparency and authenticity in their dining experiences.

Waste reduction is another critical aspect of sustainable restaurant operations. The food service industry is notorious for generating significant amounts of waste, but there are numerous strategies you can employ to minimize your environmental footprint. Begin by implementing a comprehensive recycling and composting program, ensuring that staff are properly trained on sorting procedures. Invest in reusable or biodegradable packaging for takeout orders and consider offering incentives for customers who bring their own containers. In the kitchen, implement a "nose-to-tail" or "root-to-stem" cooking philosophy, utilizing every part of an ingredient to reduce food waste and potentially create unique menu items that set your restaurant apart from competitors.

Energy and water conservation should also be high priorities for any restaurant aiming to improve its sustainability profile. Conduct an energy audit to identify areas of high consumption and implement energy-efficient solutions such as LED lighting, smart thermostats, and Energy Star-certified appliances. Install low-flow faucets and toilets to reduce water usage and consider implementing a greywater system to recycle water from sinks and dishwashers for use in landscaping or cleaning. These measures not only reduce your environmental impact but can also lead to significant cost savings over time, improving your bottom line while demonstrating your commitment to sustainability.

Engaging your staff and customers in your sustainability efforts is crucial for long-term success. Develop a comprehensive training program that educates employees on the importance of sustainable practices and their role in implementing them. Encourage staff to contribute ideas for improving sustainability, fostering a sense of ownership and pride in your restaurant's efforts. Communicate your sustainability initiatives to customers through menu descriptions, signage, and social media, highlighting the positive impact of their dining choices. Consider partnering with local environmental organizations or participating in community events to further demonstrate your commitment and build positive relationships within your community.

As you implement these sustainable practices, it's important to track and measure your progress. Establish key performance indicators (KPIs) related to waste reduction, energy consumption, and sustainable sourcing, and regularly review these metrics to identify areas for improvement. Consider pursuing certifications, which can provide valuable guidance on best practices and serve as a credible way to communicate your commitment to sustainability to customers and stakeholders.

Implementing sustainable practices in your restaurant is not without its challenges. Initial costs for energy-efficient equipment or sustainable packaging can be higher, and sourcing sustainable ingredients may require adjustments to your supply chain. However, the long-term benefits – both financial and reputational – often outweigh these initial hurdles. By taking a strategic, incremental approach to sustainability, you can manage costs while steadily improving your restaurant's environmental performance and appeal to an increasingly eco-conscious customer base.

As the restaurant industry continues to evolve, sustainability will only become more critical to success. By taking proactive steps to implement sustainable practices now, you position your restaurant as a leader in responsible business practices, potentially gaining a competitive edge in a crowded market. Remember that sustainability is an ongoing journey, not a destination. Continuously seek out new innovations and best practices and be willing to adapt your approach as new technologies and opportunities emerge. By doing so, you'll not only contribute to a healthier planet but also build a more resilient, forward-thinking business that's well-equipped to thrive in the changing landscape of the restaurant industry.

Preparing for the Future

The restaurant industry is in a constant state of flux, with new challenges and opportunities emerging at an unprecedented pace. To thrive in this dynamic environment, restaurant owners and managers must adopt a proactive approach to future-proofing their businesses. This involves developing strategies that not only address current issues but also anticipate and prepare for potential future disruptions. By building flexibility and resilience into your business model, you can ensure that your restaurant remains competitive and successful in the face of changing market conditions, consumer preferences, and technological advancements.

One of the most effective ways to future-proof your restaurant is to cultivate a culture of innovation within your organization. This means encouraging your team to think creatively, experiment with new ideas, and stay informed about industry trends. Regularly hold brainstorming sessions with your staff to generate fresh concepts for menu items, service improvements, or operational efficiencies. Create a system for evaluating and implementing the most promising ideas, and reward employees who contribute to the innovation process. By fostering an environment that values creativity and forward-thinking, you'll be better positioned to adapt to new challenges and capitalize on emerging opportunities in the restaurant industry.

Investing in versatile technology infrastructure is another crucial aspect of preparing your restaurant for the future. Rather than simply adopting the latest trendy gadgets, focus on implementing flexible systems that can easily integrate with new technologies as they emerge. For example, choose a point-of-sale (POS) system that offers regular software updates and has the capability to connect with various third-party applications. This will allow you to seamlessly incorporate new features and functionalities as they become available, without the need for costly overhauls of your entire system. Additionally, consider investing in cloud-based solutions for data storage and management, as these offer greater scalability and accessibility compared to traditional on-premises systems.

Diversifying your revenue streams is a powerful strategy for building resilience into your restaurant business model. While your core dining experience should remain the focus, explore additional avenues for generating income that can help sustain your business during challenging times. This might include developing a robust takeout and delivery program, creating a line of packaged food products for retail sale, or offering cooking classes and culinary experiences. By expanding your offerings, you'll be better equipped to weather economic downturns or shifts in consumer behavior that might negatively impact traditional dine-in services. So, these additional revenue streams can provide valuable insights into customer preferences and market trends, further informing your future business decisions.

Sustainability should be a key consideration in your future-proofing efforts, as environmental concerns continue to gain prominence among consumers and regulators alike. Implement eco-friendly practices throughout your operations, from sourcing ingredients to managing waste. This might involve partnering with local farmers to reduce your carbon footprint, implementing energy-efficient equipment and lighting, or developing a comprehensive recycling and composting program. Not only will these initiatives help you comply with increasingly stringent environmental regulations, but they can also appeal to environmentally conscious consumers and potentially reduce your operating costs in the long run.

Investing in your team's skills and knowledge is paramount to building a resilient restaurant business. Develop a comprehensive training program that goes beyond basic job requirements and focuses on developing adaptable, multi-skilled employees. Offer cross-training opportunities that allow staff to learn different roles within the restaurant, making your workforce more flexible and capable of handling various challenges. Additionally, provide ongoing education about industry trends, new technologies, and evolving customer expectations. By nurturing a knowledgeable and versatile team, you'll be better prepared to navigate future changes in the restaurant landscape and maintain high-quality service standards.

Establishing strong relationships with a diverse network of suppliers is crucial for future-proofing your restaurant against potential supply chain disruptions. Rather than relying on a single source for key ingredients or equipment, cultivate partnerships with multiple vendors. This approach not only provides you with backup options in case of shortages or quality issues but also gives you greater negotiating power and the ability to quickly adapt to changing market conditions. Consider working with local producers and artisans to create unique menu offerings and support your community, while also reducing your dependence on long-distance supply chains that may be more vulnerable to disruptions.

Regularly conducting market research and staying attuned to consumer trends is essential for anticipating future changes in the restaurant industry. Implement systems for gathering and analyzing customer feedback, such as post-dining surveys or social media monitoring tools. Use this data to identify emerging preferences and potential areas for improvement in your offerings. Additionally, keep a close eye on broader societal trends that may impact dining habits, such as shifts in dietary preferences, work patterns, or social behaviors. By staying informed and responsive to these changes, you can proactively adjust your menu, service model, or marketing strategies to meet evolving customer expectations.

Financial preparedness is a critical component of future-proofing your restaurant business. Develop a comprehensive financial strategy that includes building cash reserves, maintaining good credit, and exploring diverse funding options. Set aside a portion of your profits during successful periods to create a financial cushion that can help you weather unexpected challenges or invest in new opportunities. Establish relationships with multiple financial institutions and explore alternative funding sources, such as crowdfunding or restaurant-specific lenders, to ensure you have access to capital when needed. Regularly review and update your financial projections, taking into account potential future scenarios and their impact on your business.

Recap and Actionable Steps

The restaurant industry stands at the cusp of a technological revolution, with emerging trends and innovations reshaping the way we conceptualize, operate, and experience dining establishments. From artificial intelligence-driven kitchen management systems to augmented reality menus, the future of restaurants is brimming with possibilities that were once confined to the realm of science fiction. These advancements, while exciting, also present a unique set of challenges for restaurant owners and managers who must navigate this rapidly evolving landscape while maintaining the core essence of hospitality that defines the industry.

As we've explored throughout this chapter, staying ahead of the curve is not just about adopting the latest gadgets or jumping on every trending bandwagon. It's about understanding the underlying shifts in consumer behavior, recognizing the growing importance of sustainability, and strategically integrating technologies that enhance both operational efficiency and guest experience. The successful restaurants of tomorrow will be those that can seamlessly blend innovation with tradition, creating experiences that are both cutting-edge and comfortingly familiar.

One of the most significant insights we've gleaned is the increasing demand for personalization in dining experiences. Customers are no longer satisfied with one-size-fits-all service; they crave unique, tailored interactions that make them feel valued and understood. This shift necessitates a reevaluation of how we collect, analyze, and utilize customer data. Implementing robust Customer Relationship Management (CRM) systems, coupled with AI-powered analytics, can provide invaluable insights into individual preferences, allowing restaurants to craft bespoke experiences that keep patrons coming back for more.

Sustainability has emerged as another critical factor shaping the future of the restaurant industry. As environmental concerns continue to grow, customers are increasingly gravitating towards establishments that demonstrate a genuine commitment to eco-friendly practices. This goes beyond simply offering organic menu items or eliminating plastic straws; it encompasses every aspect of restaurant operations, from sourcing ingredients to managing waste. Restaurants that can effectively communicate their sustainability efforts and involve customers in their green initiatives will find themselves at a significant competitive advantage in the years to come.

The rise of ghost kitchens and virtual restaurant concepts represents a paradigm shift in how we think about restaurant spaces and operations. These models, which prioritize delivery and takeout over traditional dine-in experiences, have gained tremendous traction in recent years and show no signs of slowing down. For existing restaurants, this trend presents both a challenge and an opportunity. By leveraging existing kitchen capacity to launch virtual brands or partnering with ghost kitchen operators, restaurants can expand their reach and tap into new revenue streams without the overhead costs associated with traditional expansion.

As we look to integrate these insights into our business strategies, it's crucial to approach the process methodically and thoughtfully. Here's a step-by-step guide to help you future-proof your restaurant and capitalize on emerging trends:

1. Conduct a comprehensive technology audit: • Evaluate your current technology stack, identifying areas where outdated systems may be hindering efficiency or customer experience. • Research emerging

technologies relevant to your specific restaurant concept and target audience. • Prioritize technologies that offer the greatest potential return on investment, considering both immediate operational improvements and long-term strategic advantages.

2. Develop a data-driven personalization strategy: • Implement a robust CRM system to centralize customer data from various touchpoints (reservations, online ordering, loyalty programs, etc.). • Train staff on the importance of data collection and how to gather insights through customer interactions. • Use AI-powered analytics tools to identify patterns in customer behavior and preferences. • Create personalized marketing campaigns and menu recommendations based on individual customer profiles.

3. Enhance your sustainability initiatives: • Conduct an environmental impact assessment of your current operations. • Develop partnerships with local, sustainable suppliers for key ingredients. • Implement a comprehensive waste reduction and recycling program. • Explore energy-efficient equipment options and renewable energy sources. • Create educational materials for both staff and customers about your sustainability efforts.

4. Explore alternative revenue streams: • Assess the feasibility of launching a virtual brand or ghost kitchen operation. • Develop a robust online ordering and delivery system, either in-house or through strategic partnerships. • Consider offering meal kits, cooking classes, or other experiential products that extend your brand beyond the restaurant walls.

• Evaluate potential licensing or franchising opportunities for successful concepts.

5. Invest in staff training and development: • Create a comprehensive training program that covers both traditional hospitality skills and emerging technologies. • Foster a culture of innovation by encouraging staff to contribute ideas for improving operations and customer experience. • Implement a mentorship program to help develop the next generation of restaurant industry leaders. • Regularly review and update your training materials to ensure they reflect the latest industry trends and best practices.

6. Cultivate a flexible and resilient business model: • Develop contingency plans for various scenarios, including economic downturns, supply chain disruptions, and public health crises. • Build strong relationships with a diverse network of suppliers to mitigate potential shortages. • Maintain a healthy cash reserve to weather unexpected challenges and capitalize on emerging opportunities. • Regularly review and adjust your business plan to reflect changing market conditions and consumer preferences.

By methodically working through these steps, you'll be well-positioned to navigate the exciting and sometimes turbulent waters of the restaurant industry's future. Remember, the key to success in this ever-evolving landscape is not just about adopting new technologies or following trends blindly. It's about thoughtfully integrating innovations that align with your core values and enhance your ability to deliver exceptional dining experiences. The future of restaurants belongs to those who can balance tradition with innovation, creating spaces that are both technologically advanced and warmly human.

Conclusion

Core Concepts Summary

Throughout this journey, we've explored the intricate tapestry of the restaurant industry, unraveling its complexities and discovering innovative approaches to age-old challenges. The core concepts we've discussed form the bedrock of a successful and sustainable restaurant business, one that not only survives but can find continued success in an ever-evolving landscape. These principles, when applied with diligence and creativity, have the power to transform your establishment from a mere eatery into a thriving hub of culinary excellence and operational efficiency.

At the heart of our exploration lies the concept of strategic management, a multifaceted approach that encompasses every aspect of your restaurant's operations. We've gone deep into the art of crafting a vision that resonates with both your team and your patrons, creating a roadmap that guides every decision and action. This strategic foundation is not a static document gathering dust on a shelf, but a living, breathing entity that evolves with your business, adapting to market trends, customer preferences, and internal dynamics.

Employee well-being emerged as a central theme, challenging the long-standing notion that high turnover is an unavoidable aspect of the restaurant industry. We've uncovered the true cost of this revolving door mentality, not just in terms of financial drain but also in its impact on team morale, customer experience, and overall operational stability. By reimagining your staff not as replaceable cogs but as valuable assets worthy of investment, you unlock a wealth of potential that can propel your restaurant to new heights of success.

Innovation, often perceived as the domain of tech startups and cutting-edge industries, has found its place in the heart of the restaurant world. We've explored how embracing technological advancements, from sophisticated POS systems to AI-driven inventory management, can streamline operations and enhance the dining experience. However, innovation in this context extends beyond gadgets and software; it's about fostering a culture of continuous improvement, where every team member feels empowered to contribute ideas and challenge the status quo.

The concept of creating a distinctive brand identity has been woven throughout our discussions, emphasizing the importance of standing out in a saturated market. We've examined how every touchpoint, from your menu design to your social media presence, contributes to a cohesive narrative that resonates with your target audience. This brand identity is not just about attracting customers; it's about creating a loyal community that sees your restaurant as more than just a place to eat, but as an integral part of their lifestyle and social experiences.

Conclusion

Financial acumen, often overlooked in the creative whirlwind of culinary pursuits, has been brought to the forefront. We've dissected the intricacies of profit margins, cost control, and strategic pricing, equipping you with the tools to navigate the financial challenges that plague many restaurants. By mastering these financial fundamentals, you're not just ensuring survival; you're paving the way for sustainable growth and expansion.

The power of data-driven decision-making has been a recurring theme, challenging the notion that gut instinct alone can guide a restaurant to success. We've explored how to harness the wealth of information at your fingertips, from customer feedback to sales trends, transforming raw data into actionable insights. This analytical approach doesn't replace creativity and intuition; rather, it enhances them, providing a solid foundation for innovation and calculated risk-taking.

Sustainability and ethical practices have emerged as non-negotiable aspects of modern restaurant management. We've gone into how adopting environmentally friendly practices and sourcing responsibly not only contributes to the greater good but also resonates with an increasingly conscious consumer base. This commitment to sustainability extends beyond ingredients and packaging, encompassing energy efficiency, waste reduction, and community engagement.

The importance of adaptability and resilience has been underscored throughout our exploration, particularly in light of recent global challenges that have rocked the restaurant industry. We've examined strategies for pivoting quickly in response to external pressures, from diversifying revenue streams to reimagining the dining experience. This flexibility, coupled with a strong foundational strategy, is what separates thriving restaurants from those that merely survive.

As we conclude this journey, it's clear that success in the restaurant industry is not about following a single formula or replicating someone else's success story. It's about understanding these core concepts, adapting them to your unique vision and circumstances, and having the courage to forge your own path. The principles we've explored are not just theoretical concepts; they are practical tools that, when wielded with skill and passion, can transform your restaurant into a beacon of culinary excellence and operational mastery.

Encouragement for Action

The restaurant industry is a dynamic and challenging field, constantly evolving and demanding adaptability from its participants. As you've journeyed through the pages of this book, you've been exposed to a wealth of strategies, insights, and innovative approaches designed to revolutionize your perspective on restaurant management. These concepts aren't just theoretical musings; they're battle-tested tactics that have the potential to transform your establishment from a struggling enterprise into a thriving, profitable venture that stands the test of time.

Implementing change can be daunting, especially in an industry as fast-paced and unpredictable as food service. You might be hesitant to shake up the status quo, fearing that any deviation from your current practices could lead to unforeseen complications or customer dissatisfaction. However, it's crucial to recognize that the greatest risk in today's competitive landscape is not taking any risks at all. By embracing the strategies outlined in this book, you're not risking it with your business; you're making a calculated investment in its future.

Consider the potential outcomes of putting these ideas into action. Imagine a restaurant where employee turnover is no longer a constant drain on your resources, where your staff feels valued, motivated, and committed to delivering exceptional service. Picture a kitchen that operates with clockwork efficiency, minimizing waste while maximizing creativity and output. Envision a dining room buzzing with satisfied customers who not only return frequently but also enthusiastically recommend your establishment to friends and family. These scenarios aren't pipe dreams; they're achievable realities for those who have the courage and foresight to implement meaningful changes.

The positive outcomes of adopting these strategies extend far beyond mere financial gains, though increased profitability is certainly a welcome benefit. By fostering a culture of innovation and employee well-being, you're creating a work environment that attracts and retains top talent in an industry notorious for its high turnover rates. This stability allows you to build a team of seasoned professionals who understand and embody your vision, resulting in a consistently high-quality dining experience for your patrons. And as your reputation for excellence grows, you'll find yourself in a position to negotiate better terms with suppliers, attract investors if expansion is on the horizon, and perhaps even explore opportunities for franchising or opening additional locations.

It's important to acknowledge that change doesn't happen overnight. Implementing new strategies requires patience, persistence, and a willingness to learn from both successes and setbacks. You may encounter resistance from long-time employees who are set in their ways or face challenges in retraining staff to adapt to new systems. However, these hurdles are temporary and pale in comparison to the long-term benefits of modernizing your approach to restaurant management. By committing to this process of transformation, you're not just improving your business; you're contributing to the evolution of the entire industry.

As you contemplate taking the first steps towards implementing these changes, remember that you're not alone in this journey. The restaurant community is filled with passionate individuals who share your commitment to excellence and innovation. Seek out mentors, join industry associations, and engage with fellow restaurateurs who have successfully navigated similar challenges. Their experiences and insights can provide invaluable guidance as you chart your course towards a more successful and sustainable future for your establishment.

The strategies presented in this book are not meant to be prescriptive solutions that work identically for every restaurant. Instead, they serve as a flexible framework that you can adapt to suit the unique needs and characteristics of your business. Take the time to carefully evaluate each concept, considering how it aligns with your restaurant's values, target demographic, and long-term goals. This thoughtful approach will allow you to create a customized implementation plan that maximizes the impact of these strategies while staying true to your establishment's identity.

As you embark on this transformative journey, maintain an open mind and be prepared to iterate on your approach. The restaurant industry is constantly evolving, and what works today may need adjustment tomorrow. By cultivating a mindset of continuous improvement and adaptability, you'll be well-equipped to navigate the challenges and opportunities that lie ahead. Remember, every successful restaurateur was once in your position, facing the decision to either embrace change or cling to the familiar. Those who chose to innovate and evolve are the ones who have not only survived but thrived in this competitive industry.

The time for action is now. The concepts and strategies you've learned have the power to revolutionize your restaurant, but only if you have the courage to put them into practice. Start small if necessary, implementing changes incrementally to build momentum and confidence. Celebrate each success, no matter how minor it may seem, and use any setbacks as learning opportunities to refine your approach. With dedication, perseverance, and a willingness to embrace new ideas, you have the potential to transform your restaurant into a beacon of excellence in the industry, setting new standards for quality, innovation, and customer satisfaction.

Step-by-Step Actionable Takeaways

The restaurant industry is a complex ecosystem where success hinges on a delicate balance of strategic management, employee satisfaction, and innovative thinking. Throughout this book, we've explored numerous strategies and concepts designed to revolutionize your approach to running a successful restaurant. Now, it's time to consolidate these ideas into a comprehensive, actionable plan that you can implement immediately to drive positive change in your establishment.

First and foremost, let's address the cornerstone of any thriving restaurant: your team. Implementing a robust employee retention strategy is crucial for reducing turnover costs and maintaining a stable, skilled workforce. Begin by conducting a thorough assessment of your current workplace culture. Are your staff members genuinely happy? Do they feel valued and appreciated? If not, it's time to make some changes. Start by implementing a structured feedback system where employees can voice their concerns and suggestions without fear of repercussion. This could be in the form of anonymous surveys, regular one-on-one meetings, or even a suggestion box. The key is to create an environment where open communication is not just encouraged but celebrated.

Once you've established a channel for feedback, it's time to act on it. Develop a comprehensive training program that addresses the skills gaps identified by your team. This isn't just about teaching them how to perform their jobs more effectively; it's about investing in their personal and professional growth. Consider partnering with local culinary schools or industry experts to offer specialized workshops. Implement a mentorship program where seasoned staff members can guide and support newer employees. By demonstrating a commitment to your team's development, you're not only improving their skills but also fostering a sense of loyalty and belonging that can significantly reduce turnover rates.

Next, let's focus on optimizing your operations to maximize efficiency and profitability. Conduct a thorough analysis of your menu, identifying which items are your top performers and which ones might be dragging down your profits. Use this information to streamline your offerings, focusing on dishes that not only sell well but also have healthy profit margins. Don't be afraid to get creative here – consider introducing seasonal specials that take advantage of locally sourced, in-season ingredients. This not only keeps your menu fresh and exciting but can also help reduce food costs and support local suppliers.

In tandem with menu optimization, it's crucial to implement a robust inventory management system. Invest in software that allows you to track ingredient usage in real-time, helping you minimize waste and prevent overstocking. Train your staff to use this system effectively, emphasizing the importance of accurate data entry. Regularly review your inventory reports to identify trends and adjust your purchasing accordingly. This level of precision in your inventory management can lead to significant cost savings over time, directly impacting your bottom line.

Now, let's turn our attention to marketing and customer engagement. In today's digital age, having a strong online presence is non-negotiable. If you haven't already, create a user-friendly website that showcases your menu, ambiance, and any unique selling points of your restaurant. Implement an online reservation system to make it easy for customers to book tables. Develop a social media strategy that goes beyond just posting photos of your dishes. Engage with your followers, respond to reviews (both positive and negative), and use these platforms to tell your restaurant's story. Consider partnering with local food bloggers or influencers to expand your reach and attract new customers.

To truly stand out in a crowded market, focus on creating memorable experiences for your guests. This goes beyond just serving great food. Train your front-of-house staff in the art of hospitality, emphasizing the importance of personalized service. Implement a customer relationship management (CRM) system to track guest preferences and special occasions. Use this information to add personalized touches to their dining experience – a complimentary dessert for a birthday celebration or remembering a regular customer's favorite wine. These small gestures can turn first-time diners into loyal patrons who not only return frequently but also recommend your restaurant to others.

Conclusion

Sustainability is another area where you can differentiate your restaurant while also contributing to a greater cause. Develop a comprehensive sustainability plan that addresses everything from sourcing ingredients to waste management. Partner with local farms to source fresh, seasonal produce. Implement a composting program for food waste and switch to biodegradable takeout containers. Not only will these initiatives appeal to environmentally conscious consumers, but they can also lead to cost savings in the long run.

Finally, never underestimate the power of continuous learning and adaptation. The restaurant industry is constantly evolving, and staying ahead of the curve is crucial for long-term success. Make it a habit to regularly attend industry conferences, read trade publications, and network with other restaurateurs. Encourage your team to bring new ideas to the table and be open to experimenting with innovative concepts. Whether it's embracing new technology, trying out a pop-up concept, or collaborating with other local businesses, maintaining a spirit of innovation will keep your restaurant fresh and exciting for both your staff and your customers.

By implementing these actionable steps, you're not just running a restaurant; you're creating a thriving ecosystem that benefits your employees, delights your customers, and contributes positively to your community. Remember, success in the restaurant industry isn't just about serving great food – it's about creating an experience that resonates with people on multiple levels. With dedication, creativity, and a willingness to adapt, you can transform your restaurant into a beacon of excellence in your local culinary scene.

Call to Action

The journey of transforming your restaurant doesn't end with the final page of this book. It's merely the beginning of a new chapter in your professional life, one that promises growth, innovation, and success in an industry that's as challenging as it is rewarding. The strategies, insights, and practical advice shared throughout these pages are designed to be your compass in navigating the complex world of restaurant management, but their true power lies in their application.

To truly harness the potential of what you've learned, it's crucial to take the next step. Consider attending industry-specific workshops that go deeper into the concepts we've explored. These interactive sessions provide invaluable opportunities to engage with experts, share experiences with peers, and gain hands-on practice implementing new strategies. Workshops focusing on topics like innovative menu design, advanced customer service techniques, or cutting-edge marketing strategies can offer fresh perspectives and actionable insights that build upon the foundation laid in this book.

For those seeking personalized guidance tailored to their unique restaurant challenges, advisory services can be an invaluable resource. Expert consultants bring years of industry experience and a wealth of knowledge to the table, offering customized solutions that address your specific needs. You can find us at www.benchmarksixty.com to learn more about how we help restaurants navigate the challenges of business model design, labor cost management and menu optimization.

Whether you're grappling with staff retention issues, looking to optimize your operational efficiency, or aiming to revamp your entire business model, an advisor can provide the targeted support and expertise needed to turn your vision into reality. These professionals can work alongside you to develop and implement strategies that align with your goals, helping you navigate obstacles and capitalize on opportunities unique to your establishment.

In today's digital age, online resources offer a wealth of information at your fingertips. Our website, www.benchmarksixty.com, serves as a hub for continuous learning and community engagement. Here, you'll find regularly updated articles, case studies, and industry trends that complement and expand upon the topics covered in this book. The site also features opportunity to seek advice on implementing the strategies you've learned. Additionally, we offer a series of webinars hosted by industry experts, covering a range of topics from advanced financial management to innovative marketing techniques and labor cost management tailored specifically for restaurants.

For those looking to dive even deeper, our advanced online courses provide comprehensive, in-depth training on specific aspects of restaurant management. These self-paced programs allow you to expand your knowledge and skills in areas like menu engineering, staff training and development, or sustainable restaurant practices. Each course is designed to provide practical, actionable knowledge that you can immediately apply to your business, helping you stay ahead of industry trends and continuously improve your operations.

To stay connected and receive regular updates, industry insights, and exclusive content, consider subscribing to our publications on our website or social media channels. These curated resources deliver the latest trends, success stories, and practical tips directly to your inbox, ensuring you remain at the forefront of restaurant innovation. Additionally, following our social media channels on platforms like LinkedIn, can provide daily doses of inspiration, quick tips, and opportunities to engage with a community of like-minded professionals.

For immediate support or to discuss how we can assist you in implementing the strategies outlined in this book, our team of expert advisors is just a phone call away. Reach out to us at info@benchmarksixty.com to schedule a conversation. Our advisors are experienced restaurant professionals who can provide personalized guidance, answer your questions, and help you develop a roadmap for success tailored to your unique situation.

Remember, the most successful restaurant owners and managers are those who never stop learning and adapting. By taking advantage of these resources and committing to ongoing education and improvement, you're not just investing in your business – you're investing in your future and the future of the entire restaurant industry. The concepts and strategies you've learned are powerful tools, but their true value is realized only when put into action. So, take that crucial next step, whether it's signing up for a workshop, reaching out for a consultation, or diving into our online resources. Your journey towards restaurant excellence continues, and we're here to support you every step of the way.

Recommendations

The journey of transforming your restaurant doesn't end with the last page of this book.

It's a continuous process of learning, adapting, and growing. To support you on this ongoing adventure, we've compiled a comprehensive list of resources that will help you go deeper into the concepts we've explored and stay at the forefront of industry trends. These carefully curated materials range from insightful books and informative websites to professional organizations that can provide invaluable networking opportunities and support.

Let's start with some essential reading materials that will expand your knowledge base and offer fresh perspectives on restaurant management. "Setting the Table" by Danny Meyer is a must-read for anyone looking to elevate their hospitality game. Meyer's philosophy of "enlightened hospitality" has revolutionized the industry, and his book provides practical insights on creating exceptional customer experiences.

Conclusion

When it comes to staying updated with the latest industry trends and news, several websites stand out as invaluable resources. Restaurant Business Online (www.restaurantbusinessonline.com) offers a wealth of information on industry trends, technology, and best practices. Their articles cover everything from menu innovation to marketing strategies, making it a one-stop-shop for restaurant professionals. Another excellent resource is the National Restaurant Association's website (www.restaurant.org), which provides industry research, advocacy updates, and educational resources specifically tailored to the needs of restaurant owners and managers.

For those looking to dive deep into the culinary arts and innovative cooking techniques, The **Culinary Institute of America** (www.ciachef.edu) offers professional development programs and boot camps. These intensive, hands-on experiences can help you refine your culinary skills, explore new cuisines, and bring fresh ideas back to your kitchen. I have personally been a part of the Society of Fellows for the last few years, and the work that the Culinary Institute of America is doing is incredible.

Restaurants Canada also has an incredible list of resources, and they have been an amazing partner and resource for me over the years. The annual "RC Show" held in Toronto every year is a great place to connect with industry peers, find new ways of doing things, and learn about operational innovations.

Conclusion

To stay ahead of the curve in restaurant technology, the **National Restaurant Association's** NRA show (https://www.nationalrestaurantshow.com/) is an annual event that showcases the latest technological advancements and operational innovation in the industry. From mobile ordering systems to AI-powered inventory management, this summit can help you identify technologies that could streamline your operations and enhance the customer experience.

Hatch Insights (https://www.hatchinsights.ca/) is my go-to for anything data and reporting related. By equipping restaurateurs with the critical reporting and analytics necessary to stay competitive and enhance operational efficiency, it delivers value on a daily basis.

Margin Edge (https://www.marginedge.com/) has been a great partner to me, as both an operator and an advisor, and is the leader in the industry when it comes to restaurant and inventory management. The amount of time and money that the platform saves is above all others, and I cannot recommend them enough.

Open Table is our go to platform for every from sales planning based on guest count, to CRM and guest management. We use it to plan special occasion service, and we use it to understand how our guests are planning to spend their money in our restaurant.

Lastly, don't underestimate the power of local resources. Many cities have restaurant associations or hospitality alliances that offer networking events, workshops, and local market insights. These organizations can provide valuable connections with local suppliers, potential partners, and fellow restaurateurs who understand the unique challenges and opportunities in your specific market.

Remember, the key to success in the ever-evolving restaurant industry is continuous learning and adaptation. By leveraging these resources, you'll be well-equipped to navigate the challenges ahead, implement innovative strategies, and create a thriving, sustainable restaurant business that stands out in a competitive market. The journey of improvement never ends, but with these tools at your disposal, you're well-prepared to lead your restaurant to new heights of success.

Appreciations

Mom and Dad: Thank you for your unwavering support. You have both always been there for me, encouraged me, and believed in me. Through the ups and downs of life, sport and business you have always made me believe that I could accomplish whatever it was that I set out to do. Thank you.

Conclusion

Jim Stewart: From my days as a waiter in your restaurant, to today you have always shown me the importance of treating people well, protecting employee experience, and looking for opportunities to improve. There are endless leadership lessons and business strategies that I use every day which I learned from you. Thank you for over two decades of mentorship.

Kelly Higginson: I can't say enough about the leadership you show our industry and the support you have always provided me in my quest to help the restaurant industry evolve. Thank you.

Kris Hall: Few are brave enough to take the lead on matters to do with mental health, however you set the standard for how to do it. Thank you for shining a light on such an important topic in the restaurant industry. Also, thank you for allowing me to be a part of The Burnt Chef Project family.

The Restaurant Industry: I do not know where or who I would be without you. The countless lessons, the endless number of friends, the incredible experiences, crazy situations, and memories. Thank you for all that you have contributed to my life, and most importantly, thank you for bringing Jen into my life.

www.ingramcontent.com/pod-product-compliance
Lightning Source LLC
Chambersburg PA
CBHW071537200326
41519CB00021BB/6523